OPPORTUNITIES

HOW TO MAKE THE MOST OF THEM

THE TEN TITLES IN THE

MENTAL EFFICIENCY SERIES

〜

〜

FUNK & WAGNALLS COMPANY
Publishers
NEW YORK AND LONDON

OPPORTUNITIES

HOW TO MAKE THE MOST OF THEM

By L. CHARLEY

TRANSLATED BY L. O'ROURKE, M.A.

—————

AUTHORIZED EDITION   57348

—————

*"Opportunity knocks at least once at every man's door;
it is the deaf and the irresolute that it passes by."*

FUNK & WAGNALLS COMPANY
NEW YORK   LONDON
1916

PREFACE

To some readers of this book the word Opportunity may serve to recall the immortal lines penned by WILLIAM SHAKESPEARE—"There is a tide in the affairs of men, which, taken at the flood, leads on to Fortune." True as this may be, in part, the reader of these pages will not find it amiss to bear in mind that there is a *turn* to every tide, and that while some tides wash us up high and dry, leaving us in affluence on the banks of El Dorado, others take us out far beyond our depths and leave us to the mercy of the rude stream that may hide us for ever.

As the author of this book, Mr. L. CHARLEY teaches us that in this life the advantages which we obtain bear a direct proportion to the exertions which we put forth to secure them. He takes as his motto, "Opportunity knocks at least once at every man's door; it is the deaf and the irresolute that it passes by." So as to better present his subject he, at the outset, compares and contrasts Chance, Hazard, Fortune, and Luck. He shows, also, the relation of Luck to Fetishism, and discusses the part which Fortune plays in life. Even tho the mines of knowledge have often been laid bare by the divining-rod of Chance—the hazel-wand of fetishism—it must not be forgotten that Providence gives us Chance, and that man must mold it to his advantage. Altho Fortune befriends the bold, every one may be the architect of his own fortune if he makes use of his advantages. Great opportunities come to all, and the secret of success in life is to be ready to grasp them when they arrive. It was AUSTIN PHELPS' belief that vigilance in watching Opportunity; tact and daring in seizing upon Opportunity; force and persistence in crowding Opportunity to its utmost of possible achievement—these are the martial virtues that command Success.

One of England's famous orators of the last century—the EARL OF DERBY—declared that opportunity came sooner or later to all who worked and *wished*. This does not mean that he who goes about with open mouth wishing for the ripest cherries is to be the only one to receive the choicest fruits that fall from the trees. One must *work* as well as wish. "If you want to succeed in the world," said an orator of quite another stamp, JOHN B. GOUGH, "you must *make your own opportunities* as you go on. The man who waits for some seventh wave to toss him on dry land will find that that seventh wave is a long time coming." Like Dr. Matthews, the eminent author of "Getting on in the World," Mr. Charley believes that unless a man has trained himself for his opportunity, the opportunity when it comes will serve only to make him ridiculous. To every man each opportunity is worth exactly what he is prepared to make of it—so much but no more. For this reason, Mr. Charley admonishes every one of us to watch our opportunity and to grasp it when it comes, for then is the golden moment in which we may reap the reward of our efforts.

Mr. Charley discusses the possibility of outward influences conducing to fortune, but, like his famous forerunner, Bacon, implicitly believes that the mold of every man's fortune is in his own hands. He advocates the views so tersely exprest by Franklin in these words, "To be thrown upon one's own resources, is to be cast into the very lap of fortune; for our faculties then undergo a development and display an energy of which they were previously unsusceptible." The Reader who looks for success must be ever vigilant. Alert to all opportunities, he must descry them at a distance, observe their approach toward him, prepare to receive them, and as they advance grasp them as he would the hand of his dearest friend, for his hour has struck and Fortune stands at the threshold.

THE PUBLISHERS.

CONTENTS

CHAPTER I

WHAT IS FORTUNE?

BELIEF in fortune, or luck, is a relic of superstition, reviving vaguely in the mind of man the idea of Fate.

Those who regard themselves as pawns of fortune like to represent it to themselves as something obscure, yet predominant. They allow it the power of constraining events so that they must needs bend to the laws of a destiny whose decrees are inscribed, so to speak, in the book of fate. To be lucky (*avoir la veine*) signifies for them the reaching without difficulty of the goal of their hopes. It means, further, to participate in the benefits dispensed by some event, as advantageous as it is undeserved, without having made any effort to bring it about.

Luck, or good fortune, consists in the unsuspected occurrence of some favorable event.

In another phase, it is the manifestation of an unexpected solution of a problem of which the issue can not be precisely determined.

Chance (*hasard*) sometimes stamps itself so

deeply upon the physiognomy of things that many have been wont to clothe it with a sort of personality, and have given it a name. They like to represent chance as a smiling divinity, capricious and fantastic withal, something that can be startled by a mere nothing, that takes flight upon the instant, and as suddenly returns. They think that it is blind, and accuse it of favoritism if it seems to concern itself with other's interests.

If, on the contrary, it turns in their own direction they rarely recognize the fact. On the part of some this faint blindness is still mere superstition.

To acknowledge that you have been visited by fortune seems to the superstitious a sort of bravado in the face of destiny. They contend that the established fact of prosperity is enough to awaken from their sleep the evil forces resident in things. This is why it is not an infrequent thing to deny luck to those who may well be thankful for its benefits.

We have had occasion to use the word prosperity; it is often used in the sense of luck, but it never conveys the idea of unexpected success.

The word luck has a number of synonyms. The principal ones are: chance, prosperity, fortune.

There are circumstances in which their employment is a matter of indifference; nevertheless, they do not always carry the same meaning, and there are cases in which one can not be substituted for another without altering the idea intended to be conveyed.

Chance takes its name from a game played with thimbles; it comes from *chéance* (act of falling), a term that designates the point the thimble strikes in its descent.

Chance is almost synonymous with *luck,* when employed in a favorable sense.

One will say indifferently: "I have had great luck," or "Chance has favored me very much," if his intention is to convey that he has participated in some prosperous undertaking.

Of a man who is invariably successful, one says: "Chance favors him unusually," or, "His luck is on an unusual scale."

But tho one may say, "His chances of success are bad," we are not right in saying, "He has bad luck."

The word luck is only applied in a positive sense.

One may say: "He has had the luck to succeed in this affair, altho there was every chance that he would miscarry."

But one can not, of course, say: "He had the chance to succeed in this affair, altho there was every luck that he would miscarry."

Chance involves an alternative.

It can be favorable, or the contrary.

Luck can only be beneficent.

Chance and luck are the result of some event that must have been brought about in quite different, or even opposite, ways.

This event involved two chance happenings, one good, the other bad, and the exclusion of the latter in favor of the former constitutes what we call good fortune or luck.

Perhaps this term is employed a little more familiarly than the term chance, but in the favorable sense it awakens the same ideas.

We have had the chance, or the luck, to succeed well.

We have chanced or been lucky enough to meet some friend.

Employed in the plural, the word *chance* can not be replaced by the word *luck*, since it implies doubt or probability.

If we say, "the chances are this man will succeed," we mean that the man may, indeed, succeed, but also he may fail; we can not, of course, say "the luck is this man will succeed."

But we may say, "he has the luck or the good fortune to succeed," because the phrase contains no uncertainty.

Chance in the plural speaks of hope.

Luck or fortune speaks only of realization.

It does not imply fear; that is why it always designates a past or present state, never a future state.

The representation, luck, gives an image more precise, more rude, of the manifestation of the hazard that turns out happily.

The idea conveyed by chance is applied to probabilities and calculations.

We say, "I do not know whether I shall succeed, but I am going to run the chance."

This is equivalent to saying, "There are as many reasons in favor of success as there are against it."

If realization comes to give the preponderance to the influences which are favorable, then we say, naturally, "I have had the luck to succeed."

The superstitious apply the word luck to the supervention of circumstances brought about without regard to volition; they designedly exclude ability in order to lay the whole stress upon chance.

Prosperity, on the contrary, if it also be made

to include success produced by circumstances as lucky as fortuitous, presents the idea of happiness as something flowing from the cleverness that brought it about.

If it be remarked of some one, "Prosperity attends all his undertakings," one is not given to understand that his efforts have gone for nothing in the achievement. This sort of appreciation is a kind of crowning of assiduity, sagacity, and good sense, with the understanding, however, that these virtues have been powerfully aided by the beneficent course of events.

The word prosperity, like the word luck, is only used in the positive sense.

Tho one may say, "By evil chance I have encountered such and such obstacles," one can not, of course, in the same circumstances speak of "evil prosperity."

This qualification can be but rarely applied to luck (*la veine*), and, if ever, in another sense.

The expression, *avoir la veine,* came into use in the last century during the time of the gold fever in California, when there took place a general rush toward the gold-fields. It is used figuratively, and expresses the idea of luckiness in *having* found *the vein.*

The vein (of gold) denotes that portion of

the rock which differs from the rest in its composition. The word *filon* (thread) is also used to designate a portion of precious metal which like a sort of thread traverses the rest of the worthless matter. These threads radiate through the rock as do the veins in the human body, hence the application.

One may dig for days in a vein without encountering this thread, the object of all the toil; once found it must never be lost sight of, but must be followed up in all its meanderings. In such a case they used to say, "*We have struck the vein.*"

By analogy, therefore, they came to regard as "lucky chance" what reveals itself momentarily in the midst of more or less painful circumstances.

It happened at times that a miner fell upon a vein of gold which as suddenly disappeared from view, never to be found. Thereupon the toiler exhausted himself in futile efforts. He had come upon a bad vein.

We see from this instance why we can not use the formula, "bad prosperity," altho we may with propriety use the terms, "a bad vein," "evil chance," "evil fortune."

Fortune is always taken in the sense of des-

VII.2

tiny, and we look upon it as being favorable or the opposite. But the word employed without qualification always implies a prosperous condition. To affirm wealth we say, "He has made a fortune," or "*He has struck it rich*," or "Chance has favored him."

We use these words just as we use the word prosperity, without qualification, in the sense of success.

A book that has the distinction known as style is one in which the terminology has been chosen with cleverness.

A picture, a symphony, which is marked by happy inspiration is an achievement which must have been as fortunate in its conception as in its execution.

At times we say: "By happy chance I arrived on time." Under the same circumstances we may also say, "Through luck." Nevertheless, there is a shade of difference in the expressions.

To arrive on time *by a happy chance* signifies that, in spite of circumstances which might have been adverse, we have reached our destination at the right moment.

To arrive on time *through luck* implies that chance alone brought about the arrival at the opportune moment.

By happy chance can also be translated: "By a series of circumstances which are as happy as they are uncertain."

By *luck* means by a series of circumstances as happy as it is unexpected.

The same difference exists between "happy inspiration" and lucky inspiration. Happy inspiration evokes the idea of favorable surroundings in which imagination delights to radiate its influence in the wished-for direction.

Lucky inspiration represents a more fugitive state of mind; it also suggests perfection, and it will be noticed that works executed under its influence approach nearer the standard of perfection.

We have remarked that the word luck can rarely be employed in an evil sense, the reason probably being that the reverse vocabulary is already rich enough. If the word ill luck represents error or effort ill directed or false in tendency, the word reverse denotes with clearness the ruin of some legitimate hope due to an unforeseen event. We dub as failures those who are visited too often by an adverse fate, with whom nothing succeeds.

In the same sense we sometimes give them the name of *guignards* (the unlucky), a word coined

from *guignon,* which signifies "mischance."
Guignon, however, signifies a more constant condition than does *déveine,* which means "reverse."

We employ the word *déveine* in speaking of an *unexpected* reverse, while we use the word *guignon* to designate a series of circumstances which seem, so to speak, to be brought together by the will of some maleficent power.

La déveine in the past tense is applied by preference to some single event, as thus: "He has had bad luck" (*il a eu de la déveine*).

When it indicates continuity, the term is always used in the present tense.

To be *en déveine* (to face reverses) is to see the failure of everything that seemed to have the right to succeed, and to know that it all happened because of events which could not be foreseen or provided against. To be *en déveine* is to find oneself in the situation of a man who, eager to bathe his feet in the cooling surf, sees the waves retreating as he advances and always falling short of his reach.

To be *en guigne* has the same meaning.

This word comes from *guignon,* now almost obsolete.

Using analogy, the mother-wit of the Parisians

has made of this expression a play on words to indicate *déveine*, or ill luck, using the name of a species of fruits in which is classed the *guigne*.

In those circles more concerned with picturesque style than with academic expression, they call ill luck *La Cerise* (the cherry), for the reason, probably, that *guigne* comes from the French word for cherry. Poets have referred to it as "the goddess with hollow eyes," while others speak of it as a woman "of green visage." The slang of the streets, with the intimate knowledge of fact that characterizes the formation of this language, classes it under the name *La collante* (the sticker), by extension, *La poisse* (the detective bureau), because t is unrelenting.

These designations, furthermore, indicate the general trend to error which represents evil fortune as an enraged beast intent upon its prey, while good fortune is shown as a being lavishing her smiles upon those who have never troubled themselves to conciliate her favor.

Both beliefs are alike grounded in error.

By holding them we neglect to cultivate the qualities of strength which it is necessary to put in action in order to conquer adverse circumstances.

He who believes himself marked out by evil

fortune, and who takes to himself the epithets *déveinard* or *guignard*, comes very near to the truth—if not as regards the fanciful disgrace which he thinks attaints him, at least as regards the failure of his undertakings.

Good fortune is rarely the result of pure chance.

It is nearly always the result of a group of circumstances prepared by cleverness and brought about by perseverance.

It is not always possible to realize what an amount of will-power, prudence, and providence it costs people to have earned the name of lucky.

Chance is not the sovereign master of destiny. It is governed by forces which dominate its own, and luck, characteristic as it is, is often nothing but the result of slow and patient preparation. It is the obscure cause that we like to attribute to a fact which, nevertheless, is not independent of voluntary cause. It is a handy explanation for an event for which we do not like to take the trouble to find the real cause. If we trace luck back to its source we will frequently perceive that it is nothing more than the conclusion of a series of circumstances which the will—consciously or not—has determined.

To the classification given at the beginning of this chapter we may add the following commentary:

If what we name luck excludes all idea of intention it can be but the product of chance and is to be regarded as a varying and fluctuating thing, like chance itself.

There can, therefore, be no question of any one being marked out perpetually by evil chance.

There is no reason for regarding the *déveinards* or *guignards* as being thus marked out.

To maintain the contrary would be to pretend, as was done in antiquity, that man is subject to immovable fate. Such a view was condemned even by the men of the past, and would in our day be fatal for all generous initiative and all desire for betterment.

The world belongs to those who can conquer it, and who do not admit the existence of a capricious divinity, known as Chance, which is worth propitiating, while witholding from it absolute allegiance.

CHAPTER II

WATCH YOUR OPPORTUNITY AND FORTUNE WILL FAVOR YOU

THERE is a maxim that it would be well to carve in letters of gold in all places of public instruction:

"In proportion as the aid we receive from opportunity is uncertain and precarious that which we obtain by our own efforts is efficacious and lasting."

Appealing to fortune is too often the resort of the idle and the feeble, of those who want accomplished by chance the thing that they lack the courage to do themselves.

Circumstances, if carefully considered, are much less the product of chance or blind luck than the result of a series of incidents due to individual acts, and joined to the will-power necessary to bring them about. Those who are honest in their observation of things will nearly always perceive that the element they regard as luck in the affairs of the prosperous is mostly the consequence of long preparation. They will perceive that it is eagerness to take advantage of the lucky chance as soon as it presents itself, by taking measures all converging to the central idea, which has produced surrounding conditions favorable to seizing the impending Opportunity.

No matter how favorable Opportunity may seem, it will never abide with us if we are content to leave it to its own devices.

Opportunity is a visitor who rarely calls on those who neglect to provide a suitable welcome.

It resembles the traveler in the old German tale:

"One stormy day a rich man entered the wretched cabin of some poor peasants for shelter. The peasants were dazzled by the costly jewelry and sumptuous armor of their guest, and were fain to rejoice at the honor shown them. The traveler, however, brought along with his other luggage a goodly store of fine provisions which he allowed them to feast upon. So great was their enjoyment of these that they forgot all about the duties of hospitality. Their delight in the good things, aided by their natural indolence, caused them to neglect the making of a fire, and the guest was left to shiver in his wet clothes.

"Noticing all this, the traveler hurriedly gathered his things together and in spite of the deluge of rain departed forthwith, never to return.

"Now, the peasants had neighbors who proved to be more intelligent than they.

"Perceiving the stranger who was now approaching them, they hastened to throw vine-branches upon the hearth and invited him with smiles to come in and make himself at home among them.

"They prest around him and would not consent to partake of the provisions that he had brought until they had first made sure that he was comfortably installed.

"Revived by the pleasing warmth and touched to the heart by the fineness shown in the welcome, the traveler tasted the sweetness that comes of kind hearts and home surroundings.

"He did not leave on the morrow as he had intended to do, but prolonged his stay, and did not depart until he had by largess and solemn promises assured the future of his amiable hosts."

If we go into the philosophy of this tale we instantly perceive that the peasants first mentioned were the more favored, since it was at their door that Opportunity in the form of the traveler first knocked.

Opportunity is like this traveler.

It does not permit us to profit by its gifts unless we try to deserve them.

It instantly deserts those who are content to enjoy its benefits without making an effort to augment them by activity and intelligence. Furthermore, it should be remarked that if these qualities be treated with disdain they are in a fair way to desert their possessor for one more advised and energetic.

People who are spoken of as "having succeeded" are invariably those who have relied upon themselves and never based their hopes upon any merely lucky event.

Those who rely first of all upon themselves, without counting upon the intervention of chance, are vastly more certain of experiencing its effects than are the indolent, whose cerebral effort is limited to the desiring of some fortuitous circumstance.

To enjoy success without having to occupy oneself with the cares essential to its realization—this is the ardent desire of the incapable and of those lacking in strength of mind.

We can not repeat this often enough: What we

call luck or chance is above all a coadjutor, whose
aid the clever try to invoke even at the cost
of intelligent sacrifices. It is rarely productive
by itself, and the achievements which are due to
its sole potency are never lasting. It is a capricious thing that must first be lured and then kept
by every possible means, even by force. To prevent it from taking flight far-seeing resolves and
individual strength are more potent than any
kind of sortilege, the vagaries of which are de-
spised by sane and well-regulated minds.

There is a well-known proverb, at once naïve
and striking, which illustrates the necessity of
participating by one's own efforts in bringing
about fortunate circumstances and in giving
them permanence.

"What comes at the sound of the flute departs
at the sound of the drum."

Which is the same as saying that prosperity
which comes unexpectedly, or luck that arrives
at our door without our doing anything to summon it does not stay very long. Some caprice
brought it, some fancy made away with it. The
tones of a flute summon it; it is then tempted
by the sound of a drum and directly flies toward
the new attraction, which in turn begins to pall.

It has been remarked, in fact, that suddenly

acquired fortunes that bear no relation to merit or industry crumble away of themselves.

The reason is plain. *He who does not know the value of effort can not attach the same value to success as can he who has devoted to it a portion of his life.*

Difficulty of seeking and postponement lend all the more value to realization.

We look with disdain upon the triumphs that seem too easy and seek out those that seem beyond our reach.

Is it worth while for us to cite here the old example of supply and demand?

There are things which are beautiful and desirable in themselves whose value as merchandise is *nil* because they exist in too great quantity, and the certainty of getting them whenever we want them does away with all bother about procuring them in advance.

People who have come into possession of wealth through circumstances entirely independent of themselves rarely know how to take care of it, still less to make it fruitful.

They yield to the intoxication that comes of easy possession and make no effort to profit by their good fortune, which, in their view, is a tribute to their own merit.

It is not the same with those who have made their fortune in the various ways that human industry has put at the disposal of active natures. They have a keen remembrance of the privations incident to the first savings; for them every coin is an eloquent reminder.

The first hundred-dollar-bill which they were able to set aside from what is needed for household maintenance means an epoch in their existence; and they recall, not without feeling, the day when they were able to think of the possibility of old age free from material cares and consecrated to noble projects, which, like a nimbus, will surround their final years with honor and serenity.

They are careful never to make any ill use of their good fortune. The remembrance of all the efforts that it cost to make it serve them confirms them in the resolution to make the most of its gifts and to conserve its favor. Remembrance of hopes, inconveniences, struggles, nerves them to provide against their repetition and, if it be impossible to forestall ill luck, its evil effects can be neutralized in some sort by the adoption of adequate measures.

Opportunity, however great, has no real efficacy unless it is buttressed by activity—which is its main support.

It does not like to be treated as a dupe, and it is chary of its favors save to those who know how to second them by genuine collaboration. It has a horror of the clumsy and the indolent, and quickly turns away from the light-minded who never second its efforts in their behalf.

The diversity of form which it assumes is at times deceiving, and under certain aspects it can only be recognized by the intelligent.

The superficial do not always perceive the *rôle* which it is possible for them to play in the course of events, and they remain indifferent spectators of those things which, could they avail themselves of them, might become for them the agents of prosperity.

Numberless are the dreamers who are seeking to store up the sun and who imagine that they have made a conquest of its rays when they have imprisoned them in the vase which they illumine.

Alas! winter has arrived, and they sit shivering before the empty hearth; the beneficent rays they thought so safely stored have vanished.

Those, on the other hand, whose minds are of a subtler fiber, and who do not recoil from active collaboration, go much deeper into the subject. They have knowledge of the caloric strength of the sun rays, and bring to this potency the addition of their own industry, in order to put them to the best advantage.

Some plant trees which, vivified by the sun, become, as it were, the incarnation of its jocund fires, under whose protecting influence the assembled family taste the joys of physical wellbeing and the blessings of love and home.

Others attract the clear, warm rays into greenhouses where rare flowers, under the action of the sun, aided by human toil, are seen in fullblown beauty, and become for their owners a source of sweetness and a means of subsistence.

In this the learned find a great source of pleasure and instruction for all.

Opportunity, without cooperation, may be regarded as a transient and isolated circumstance, produced without reason and without motive for renewal. There are cases, even, when its intervention may be considered unfortunate.

If it show itself at the opening of a career, if some circumstance which can not possibly be foreseen open wide the portals of success without any one having to provide the necessary machinery, there are strong reasons for believing there will result an evil influence upon the future of the supposed beneficiary.

The one who enters without firing a shot the place which others have besieged for long months will always ignore the difficulties rising in his path and, dizzy with his initial success, will rear up before the first obstacle that presents itself.

Knowing nothing of the difficulties that beset all beginnings, he will be the less likely to persevere, and the goal which he will try to reach will be a wholly different one from that to which he should try to attain.

On the other hand, he who has striven against the uncertainties and complexities that harass nearly all beginnings will look upon each step forward as a victory gained, will regard each realized project as something to be capitalized in view of the supreme achievement.

There are persons who have been known actually to thank their ill luck upon occasion; and, wholly paradoxical as this seems, it is not difficult to comprehend their position. The thing, indeed, is worth analyzing.

Upon certain apathetic natures what is called ill luck may have valuable results.

Necessity for reaction, obligation to tear oneself from the delights of *far niente* by creating the need of activity, vivifies individual energy, which but too frequently lies dormant in the time of prosperity.

Now not to go forward means to lose ground.

He who settles down in complete satisfaction with the lot which fortune has assigned him, and who puts forth no effort to cooperate with this invaluable adjunct, need not count upon the constant intervention of fortune.

One evening, as Tagliani was leaving the stage wholly overcome at the triumph of her reception, an obscure little *danseuse* addrest these words to her:

"Ah! how fortunate you are."

"True," said the star, "but I make the most of my good fortune."

"Ah!" cried her little actress-friend, much interested, "you have some special means, some talisman, perhaps?"

"I have, indeed," said Tagliani, smiling.

"How I should love to know what it is!"

"Come around to-morrow and I will show it to you."

And the next day the little *danseuse* visited Tagliani. The great actress had just finished two hours of work, and was so completely worn out that her visitor saw her sinking into the arms of her father, who was giving her her lesson. He was laying her upon a sofa and trying to revive her with a cordial.

Opening her eyes Tagliani met those of her comrade.

"You see now," she said. "Behold my talisman. It is *Work*!"

And she added: "You have all the means of acquiring this talisman; but very few of you have the strength to put it into practise."

Anecdotal history does not tell us whether the lesson proved profitable, but it is likely that it had as much effect upon her who received it as such lessons generally have.

The usual attitude of those who feel themselves incapable of the effort which the successful make is found in such remarks as: "Oh, I could never do anything like that!" And they set themselves in quest of luck without perceiving that they are acting exactly as if they were trying to repel it.

Desire for Opportunity can be a stimulant, but unaided aspiration can not be of value.

Fortune only comes to those who regard it as an adjunct, and not as the preponderant element of affairs.

No one can say with honesty: "I have had hard luck all my life."

If such a one were sincere he would perceive that in not a few circumstances he could have brought about a change in things, had he but the courage to take hold of them in the right way.

In nearly all circumstances of life there is a good and a bad side, and the question always is how to distinguish so as not to take the wrong course and give preference to the evil over the good.

In the choice, moreover, reflection and wisdom must be brought to bear. Moral considerations must also be permitted to interweave in the decision, with a view to guarding against possible evil consequences.

It will be seen from all this that fortune plays a less considerable part in life than most persons are tempted to believe, and that it is within the reach of all to conquer ill chance by strong resistance and thus experience the truth of the title of this chapter.

Foster Opportunity and Fortune will favor you.

CHAPTER III

LUCK AND FETISHISM

ALL believers in the potency of luck are more or less given to fetishism.

They all believe in the influence of some indefinite power which takes up its residence in objects the most diverse.

For some the fetish bears a tangible aspect: it may be some charm suggestive of the conjuror's art.

Such are the coral horns which are so prized in Italy, and supposed to represent those of the prince of darkness.

That personage holds this cult in consideration, and has a special care over those who wear his emblem.

Certain of these coral ornaments have the form of a closed hand, the index and little finger being extended.

The bearers of these fetishes, upon meeting any object which would bring them bad luck, do not omit to hold out before the person or thing thus incriminated their jewel-fetish, which, by pointing its horns at the evil-bearer never fails to put it to flight.

In child-speech the principle is the same, for the gesture is termed "making horns."

Animals also enjoy this privilege, according to certain superstitious persons.

There are serious men who will not enter upon a business undertaking unless they meet a white horse before the door of the building in which the transaction is to be concluded.

If a piebald horse chances to pass they are ready to accept all the conditions which, barring this incident, they would sternly have rejected.

We see people give themselves serious trouble in order to become possest of a black cat, the pretension being that this animal brings luck.

If in despite their affairs miscarry they will declare gravely that the cat was not entirely black, but had a few silver threads in his somber coat.

The cult of frogs is quite popular in certain countries. They are worn for adornment; to murder a frog involves the idea of imminent misfortune.

Words, also, in the view of fetishists, have the power of evoking bad luck. Where is the cavalryman who would let fall a "Good luck!" on departing without showing slight signs of vexation?

It is not in Italy alone that the "evil eye" is dreaded.

Many who seem otherwise well-balanced are disturbed by the presence of any one to whom they attribute malign influence.

They will say: "I don't want to go to this reception because I shall meet some one there who will bring me bad luck."

And if, despite their resolution, they find themselves forced to go to the affair, they never fail to hold some "unlucky" person responsible for all the mishaps of the evening.

There are people who, without any fault of their own, find themselves objects of general reprobation because fetishists have given them the reputation of bringing "bad luck."

These observations have a bearing on certain facts or remarks. For many the simple phrase, "I am happy," is fraught with evil consequences.

Others there are who will never admit that they are in perfect health.

By declaring themselves satisfied with their lot they fear that they may rouse the evil powers which are ever watching us with envious eyes.

Most of these superstitions rest on coincidences, and these are carefully noted by minds tainted with this weakness.

Because two events take place at the same time, or nearly so, they conclude that these circumstances have a reciprocal and mysterious influence upon each other, and they accept this conclusion without trying to understand it.

With minds denuded of individual will-power, this mystery produces a burst of faith which makes the adepts think that unknown forces resident in things can be favorable if their aid be invoked.

Now, the only means of showing these powers proper respect lies in according them some real importance. And observers have long since remarked that the power of the fetish is in direct ratio with the devotion it inspires.

This apparently disconcerting fact is easily explained by the confidence which faith imparts.

Numerous examples may be cited of persons exposed to constant dangers which they usually brave successfully, who lose their heads in the face of peril if they discover they have lost some fetish which served them as a charm.

If they have but the certainty that the object of their trust is in their possession they will fearlessly accomplish the most dangerous fea

This will appear a little disconcerting to one who does not take into consideration the *rôle* which imagination plays with those destitute of moral strength.

The impression they feel may be analyzed thus:

Debility of mind.

Doubt in oneself.

Want of support.

Superstition.

Faith.

Influence exerted by Faith.

The characteristic of debility of mind is that it prevents people from believing in their own worth.

They do not appreciate, or rather they depreciate the immutable forces which are latent in every one, and the feeling they have of their helplessness forces upon them the idea of protection.

At the moment of accomplishing an act, mistrust, the enemy of all initiative, suggests doubt as regards the happy issue of their undertaking. The need for support growing in them, they buttress their hopes with everything that seems to promise aid, no matter how mysterious.

Here we have the awakening of superstition.

Once pricked on this side, imagination lends to every incident of life an importance which is redoubled by the repetition of dependent facts.

It is sufficient in this state of mind if one happens to have on his person some unusual object. Straightway he will find some relation between the trinket and the events which were coincident with his wearing it.

People will say: "This incident happened the last day I wore this ring, and it has just occurred again to-day; now, I had not worn it between times." At first the idea of coincidence prevails, but the need for outward support which rules all feeble natures inclines in the direction of superstition.

Such a person will insist on wearing the ring next day in the hope that it will bring about some happy event. If such a thing actually happens—and imagination never fails to suggest something, however unimportant, the talisman is approved in form, and superstition blends into faith whose sincerity is in proportion to its absurdity.

Now, throughout the ages it has been established that of all moral forces Faith is the most powerful. It is so, above all, with feeble natures, who hesitate to accept responsibilities and are prone to transfer them to inanimate objects.

When Mahomet's legions seemed ready to yield ground he made them achieve prodigies of valor by assuring them that legions of angels were fighting with them.

For him who feels himself the victim of moral cowardice the fetish is the mysterious helper which restores courage and gives strength to continue a fight in which the combatant feels that he is no longer alone.

Those whose intellectual education is incomplete, or those, more numerous still, for whom moral weakness interdicts reflection are always powerless to determine the relation of cause and effect.

To trace an incident to its source seems to them too painful a task; they find it much easier to see in things the results of apparent concordances which, for the most part, have no standing in fact.

One must also take into account the need for the marvelous which lies deep in the heart of man.

Infantile education has not remained indifferent to this tendency. The tales of the nursery familiarize children with fantastic visions, in which they are shown good fairies with magic wands and genii armed with talismans, who are wont to appear unexpectedly at the most critical moments of life.

Is it to be wondered at if the impressions made upon the childish minds are not entirely effaced when the adult stage is reached? Or is it astonishing that as men they should still have a yearning for the occult things and talismans that had so large a share in their childish faith?

It sometimes happens that objects regarded as fetishes may become so, thanks to the slight strength of will of those who venerate them.

In addition to fetishes of beneficent character there remain to be considered what the superstitious regard as evil talismans.

Numberless are the objects which in the common view *bring misfortune.*

Those who assure us of this base their assumptions on facts which in the eyes of those who are not experts may pass for undoubted demonstrations.

Only a careful observer can discern the truth under the tinsel of superstition that tricks it out.

From the thousand examples which may be cited we will take one.

A woman one day bought a mildewed chafing-dish at a public sale. Arrived home, she lost no time in cleaning off its yellow coating and, proud of her work, she showed her prize to her neighbors.

One of them held up the little utensil to examine it more closely and, finding a lizard in the casting, declared she recognized the object. It belonged, she averred, to one of her lodgers who had used it under tragic circumstances. The owner had lighted it near his bedside and died that night. And the gossip added:

"If I were in your place I would not keep it, *it will bring you bad luck.*" The new owner of the chafing-dish, vexed at the non-approval of her proud purchase, merely shrugged her shoulders and received the advice with contempt.

Meanwhile the warning had roused uneasiness in her. Her disquiet was increased by an incident of a very common kind.

Slightly uneasy in mind, she had gone downstairs to make preparations for the evening, without troubling to find a place for the chafingdish, which she left on the floor.

When she returned it was nightfall, and the room being dark she could not perceive the obstacle in her path and, tripping upon it, fell headlong, striking her head against the edge of a table. They ran in at her cry, and stupefaction reigned among the neighbors when the cause of the accident became known. The blow received was a severe one and resulted in serious headache. The woman thought to get relief in rest but she found it impossible to sleep.

The talking made her head buzz, the predicted evil augury followed so quickly by the reality haunted her tortured brain. Fever made its appearance and became so violent that toward morning the patient, becoming hysterical, insisted there was but one means of escaping the evil power that was afflicting her.

She rose from the bed and lighted the chafing-dish.

When the sun rose the neighbor who called to inquire how she was, found her dead from asphyxiation.

"I knew well enough this chafing-dish would bring her misfortune," cried the woman.

We have chosen this example because it certainly is an impressive one.

Nevertheless, if we examine the incident we shall find that what is called bad luck is wholly absent from all the circumstances of the case. The whole series of events is perfectly logical.

If the woman's mind had been strong enough

to react against the anxiety caused by apprehended evil she would not have neglected to take the ordinary precaution to keep the path clear and the accident and its fatal consequences could not have occurred.

Without the fall caused by her negligence there would have been no pain in the head, no fever, and no temporary derangement of reason; the definitive act would not have taken place.

If the owner of the chafing-dish had been content to smile at her neighbor's superstition and taken proper care of her acquisition nothing would have happened.

Even admitting that the fall had taken place under the same conditions, a person of strong character would simply be imprest with the fact that it was an accident.

Instead of imputing a supernatural cause to such a common occurrence the injured woman should have blamed it all upon her own stupidity.

But in no instance will any one ever admit his own insufficiency.

It is much easier to shift the fault over upon some mysterious power whose intervention seems as an excuse for indolence and incapacity.

"I'm in hard luck," is the cry of the indolent, who do nothing to get into the good graces of Fortune.

And little by little, hatred of all effort helping, they come to regard themselves as the victims of some occult evil which they try to combat by means not less mysterious.

To ill luck they oppose the fetish, without having any misgiving that this relic of idolatry is the most certain cause of their misfortune, and confident in the potency of their amulet they set themselves to reinforce it to the best of their ability.

There are, again, persons of very sedate nature who allow themselves to be tainted by belief in fetishism.

With them, however, this belief takes on the aspect of reason.

The fetish appears to them not only as a shield against evil chance but as a safeguard against doubt.

Reflection, confused by the strong need for protection which they feel, makes them contract for some assurance against their own weakness.

In their fetishism there exists a large portion of common sense.

The conception of double personality intervenes to support the decadent "ego" with the energetic "ego," to the advantage of the former.

A well-known orator of great influence in the politics of Europe never made an important speech without wearing a certain waistcoat which he reserved for contingencies of particularly delicate nature.

To some friends who rallied him upon this mania, unworthy of a great mind, he made the following confession:

"This fetishism is less unreasonable than you would be led to believe.

"By this act of superstition I render satisfaction to the psychological entity which is the 'ego' in which atavism has preserved the old leaven of idolatry that formerly ruled the thoughts of my ancestors.

"In flattering it I also appease conflicting energies so deeply buried in my soul that they only manifest their hostility by an ill-defined feeling which nevertheless gives rise to a torturing impression—doubt.

"Once at peace with its obscure antagonist, my other 'ego,' released from all fear, gives the measure of what it can accomplish."

This concession to the demands of an occult

"ego" is often the starting-point of fetishism.

But there are not many who are capable of analyzing it as did the statesman we referred to.

Rarer still, those energetic souls who know how to appease the importunate "ego" with the alms of superstition, which they themselves are the first to smile at, and who, having done this, appeal to the forces which they feel vibrating in them before entering the battle in which, thanks to their slight sacrifice to weakness, they are certain of triumph.

Fetishism, which was the initial stage of all religions, is the genesis of belief and a power superior to any human power.

Our primitive ancestors, upon beholding cataclysms of which their limited knowledge could not determine the causes, came quite naturally to attribute them to the anger of a superior power.

The idea of appeasing this overwhelming power followed upon the perception of its manifestations, and of the sentiment of fear was born fetishism.

When the means of appeasing this supreme power was thought to have been found men next tried to render it favorable to them.

The result of certain coincidences awoke in them a rudimentary sense of observation; they remarked that some happy event that took place on the day they performed a certain act was renewed on the day that act was repeated. But a single step more is required to establish belief in a strict relation between these two very different ideas; the necessity of some protecting influence did the rest, and long before the establishment of any definitive religion that of idols governed men.

In spite of the evolution determined by science, in spite of the intervention of knowledge and reason, there are to be found many people at the present time who, independently of their religious beliefs, whether real or negative, feel the need of worshiping a tangible divinity.

They therefore invent luck—or ill luck—giving it some form under which they may render it homage.

As we have said, it is at times some familiar object, at times a jewel or some article of apparel.

As for the cult of fetishism, it spreads with surprizing rapidity and passes easily from object to impression.

A person orders a carriage, and in the course

of the journey mechanically reads the number. Involuntarily he adds the two figures and the cipher thus obtained straightway becomes fatidical. If success has marked the object of the journey this numeral is raised to the rank of a fetish.

You see every day people who plume themselves on being serious deliberately seek out a *fiacre* with numerals whose addition will make the cipher 21.

Others will withdraw in terror if they chance to set foot in a carriage whose numerals produce the number 13.

All of these are the slaves of a divinity as illusive as she is capricious, namely of *Luck* whom, like the idolaters of old, they love to clothe with a sort of actuality lest she remain invisible.

Like the pagans also, they pay special reverence to the naughty goddess, of whose wrath they stand in fear.

Exorcisms against bad luck mingle in their feeble brains with invocations to good luck and determine, even in cases where the mental apparatus is healthy enough, a sort of inequilibrium made up of doubtful faith and certain doubt, of which the former is addrest to their creed and the latter to their sense of personal worth.

The unfailing result of these wanderings can not be otherwise than a weakening and arresting influence set in the path of that evolution that leads to the source of all good: *The Best* which is at once the cause and effort of perfection.

CHAPTER IV

FORTUNE FAVORS THE BOLD

AH! if I had only dared! But I knew how poor I was in luck.

How often have we all heard people give expression to this double regret—so melancholy in its terseness.

The sentiment of ill luck is, in effect, a wall, against which all efforts break and shatter.

At times it is merely the reproduction of a state of mind caused by partial failure.

But most often we must attribute it to some real fact; certain people never dare to make the attempt because up to that moment nothing has succeeded with them.

To believe blindly in their statement would be equivalent to following them in their error. Nevertheless, it is true that many men seem to have the right to take to themselves the title of *unlucky* since all that they have attempted has resulted in failure.

To the superficial observer their case seems an obvious one, for it is impossible to deny that

52

if the capricious goddess has not loaded them with her favors, neither has she afflicted them with her blows.

Also, these same persons would be greatly surprised if one were to demonstrate to them that the rigors of their lot are deserved, nay actually provoked by their own conduct.

Fortune loves not those who hesitate. She never turns toward those who refuse to dare.

Timidity is no part of the appanage of fortune's favorites; she is a venturesome goddess who loves the audacious.

She despises those who are incapable of performing an act of strength in order to win her.

All those who say, "If I had dared," and who have not dared, are right in adding that they have little luck, for they themselves acknowledge that they have done nothing to obtain it.

Daring, rightly understood, is the source of so much success that the timid covet it and attribute it to luck alone.

We have already said, and can not repeat it too often, that luck alone does not suffice for success.

Only in rare exceptions is it ever found as a spontaneous growth.

Luck is sown as plants are sown; it must be cultivated under penalty of withering; its fruits are gathered only when it has reached maturity.

Now, timidity is a parasite plant which smothers under its thick foliage the vegetables that audacity protects and supports.

Timidity is, by nature of the defect which isolates it, voluntarily removed from the scene of struggle.

Need he be astonished at not being victorious who has not taken part in the fight?

Life is a battle, and the prize of victory is for the cleverest as well as for the bravest.

This victory, according to its kind, takes the name of realization, success, or good fortune.

Realization is the terminus of the efforts directed toward the goal aimed at.

It always involves a series of labor in which are intermingled rapid decisions and accomplishments, one dependent upon the other.

It is a chain of which the first link is desire and the last satisfaction.

Success can be more rapid.

It bears at times upon a single event; at other times it constitutes a group of facts, all converging toward a principal fact.

It is also more definitive than realization in the sense that it is a synthesis.

A realization can make other realizations prosper.

A success merely leaves after it the desire to maintain or perfect itself.

It exists, like realization, at the cost of efforts more or less decisive, and demands in greater measure the qualities of daring and decision.

Opportunity, good fortune—in appearance at least—admits less of labor and seems to bring success without our doing anything to evoke it.

Certainly there occur opportunities of astonishing character which seem to affirm the declaration of those who regard chance as the sovereign master of things; these understood opportunities, however, are seldom taken advantage of by the timid who are frightened off by the duties and obligations which good fortune involves.

They do nothing to consolidate the uncertain edifice of fortune and allow it to crumble away in ruin, giving way meanwhile to their sad refrain, "I did not dare."

Most often the emergence of this kind of opportunity is due to the legitimate operations of the daring who have known how to uncover it.

The quicksand that lies in wait for the timid in their attempt to conquer fortune is not merely inaction, to which all the timid are prone by nature of their defect; it is rather ignorance, the result of isolation, which makes futile all effort to escape from their moral imprisonment.

It is not a rare thing to see men habitually timid at heart over-excited as the result of sarcasm, and perhaps jealous of what they call their neighbor's luck, fling themselves headlong into danger upon occasion, regardless of the warnings of the intelligent.

They are like children who would leap over obstacles of which they can not gage the height. If one shows them their error they will instantly reject the advice, for presumption is nearly always the defect of the timid.

The same defect may be applied to the superficial—those who confound temerity with audacity, and who glory in trying to accomplish things which are beyond their powers.

The daring often go to the length of their endowments but never beyond them.

Audacity is made up of small qualities which, tho unrecognized by the reactionaries of progress, must under modern conditions of life be counted as real virtues.

An act of daring accomplished under conditions which do not leave it open to the charge of useless temerity is produced by many determining causes:

Judgment, clear-cut, and safe.

Promptitude of decision.

Instantaneous discernment of what is merely hurtful temerity.

Will-power, which dispenses courage.

And finally ambition, which suggests the goal.

Good judgment is a trait of great potency toward which gravitates a world of qualities having an inferior, tho essential rôle.

It is an operation of the mind permitting both the exercise of control over spontaneity and the rejection of tastes and interests of least importance, with a view of laying stress on the thing that is most important.

It is the art of foreseeing even in their slightest consequences the acts that we have resolved to accomplish.

Further, it is the art of applying the principles of deduction which flow from impartial comparison.

Good judgment demands great independence of ideas and, in addition, the sagacity that comes of presence of mind.

Never has an enthusiast attained to good judgment.

His imagination will always lure him far beyond the point which should be the goal of his effort.

He will allow himself to be persuaded by fallacious arguments whose sonorous character will appeal to him, and he will spurn the wise advice offered as a counterpoise to his boyish ardor.

He who is gifted with good judgment will also avoid that stagnation of ideas which so many have made as a law unto themselves.

The principle involved is certainly respectable enough, and those who are guided by it are worthy of consideration, but they overlook the fact that between the obstinate maintaining of an opinion and error the distance is so slight that it may be passed over without one being aware of it.

How is it possible to adhere to some pet opinion when the reasons on which it is based are constantly changing in character.

The evolution of manners and of states of mind forcibly bring about the evolution of thought and, by consequence, the upheaval of principles which are at the root of all reasoning.

In order to render an impartial judgment of things it is, then, essential to permit thought to follow the bent of actual, existing ideas and to adopt the conclusions thus arrived at to the predominating sentiment of the social life of the period. Some measure that was praiseworthy twenty years ago would now earn the reprobation of opportunists.

At that time those who wanted to travel fast used carriages; now they would be distanced by automobiles, and those who are old-fashioned enough to use the former mode of locomotion must be satisfied with a place in the rear.

Good judgment should then take note of all the circumstances present in a fact, and should reject those that smack of error.

To adhere to one set of opinions is to deny progress and to repel opportunity, which does not love the obstinate and the timorous.

Perfect judgment, by accelerating the production of ideas, provokes the promptitude of decision essential to the daring act.

Habit of observation and of comparison by doing away with the tendency to accept ready-made opinions leaves to a mind naturally active the opportunity to distinguish the truth and to establish rapidly the true relations of things.

It thus becomes easy to arrive at a solution, for imagination thus solicited can readily take in the favorable possibilities of acquisition and successfully elude the undesirable ones.

This rapidity of decision permits us to discern the faint boundary which separates audacity from temerity.

Both traits tend strongly toward the same goal, but while the man of daring, thanks to the will to reason, seizes with a firm grasp the relationship of things, the man given to temerity sees only the goal of his desires and never calculates the consequences of the act which, theoretically, ought to reach the object of his solicitude.

"Two men," we read in "Timidity: How to Overcome It," "once set out to seek Fortune.

"They traversed fields and mountains without finding any trace of the capricious goddess.

"They were on the brink of despair, when one evening as the setting sun was shedding its rosy beams over the land, they reached a marsh which suddenly brought their journey to an end.

"On the farther side green plains and trees loaded with flowers beckoned them across.

"They tried every means, but the marsh was the only way of reaching the desired point.

"Now, to venture in that direction meant certain disaster; they therefore decided to retrace their steps, when suddenly they saw a form outlined against the fiery sky.

"It was *She* beyond a doubt; it was Fortune who was beckoning them onward, smiling upon them the while.

"Trembling with emotion they stood mute for a moment, their eyes fixt upon the lovely form which summoned them so invitingly.

" 'We must go to her,' they cried, 'but how.'

" 'By the shortest route,' cried one, making as if to plunge headlong.

" 'Have you lost your senses?' cried his companion, holding him back. You know well these swamps will swallow up any one that ventures into them.'

"Without deigning to listen to the warning the rash youth tore himself away and flung himself into the marsh which swallowed him as so much prey.

"In the meantime the other had gathered branches, and these he threw upon the miry surface of the marsh, arranging them with care.

"True, in doing this he risked his life, but he did not run upon certain death like his companion.

"Taking a good start he ran lightly over the branches which disappeared behind him in the mud; in a few leaps he landed upon the opposite bank.

"Fortune, who had merely smiled disdainfully upon the rash exploit of the first member of the party and was continuing on her way, paused suddenly, her attention being caught by the daring efforts of the second youth who was clever enough to seize hold of a corner of her mantle."

No comparison could show, as this story does, the difference between rashness and daring.

In the latter youth we see unfolded all the qualities that constitute daring.

Nicety of judgment is shown in the certitude that characterizes the act about to be attempted.

The daring man *knew* by dint of rapid reasoning the thing that *was necessary* to do in order to win the success which was smiling upon him from afar in the guise of Fortune.

Promptness of decision supplied him with the immediate resolution essential to accomplishing his purpose.

But *his power of discernment*, which enabled him to differentiate between audacity and temerity, enabled him to see the utter folly of any direct act; while *will which dispenses courage* joined to *ambition which suggests the aim* did not permit him to neglect the opportunity presented to him.

He now draws upon good judgment as well as upon deduction, child of experience; and his natural activity of mind coming to his aid, the means usually employed for fording a marsh immediately occurred to him.

Quick decision has lent him its powerful aid, enabling him to accomplish in turn the task which circumstances impose upon him; and daring, firm, sane, and reasoned—the only kind worth having—sustains him with its magical power. Thus equipped, he launches into the struggle assured of victory.

All the mystery of luck is often thus explained.

The superficial, those who are victims of their own mental shallowness, devotees of superstition, will see in such cases nothing but brilliant tricks of Fortune.

They reason this way: The first man dies and the second makes his fortune; the latter is a lucky man, and one to be envied. As for the first, they can not sufficiently deplore his fate. They regard him as a victim of *bad luck,* altho, as we see, his fate was due directly to faulty judgment which prompted him to an act of absurd temerity that could have no other than a lamentable result.

It still remains to speak of ambition, a trait which plays so important a rôle in all acts of daring.

This trait is a phase of pride which can not be too highly prized since it is the most telling manifestation of desire for betterment—a trait which may conduce to the realization of the finest projects.

Ambition constitutes a sword and buckler against the invasion of mediocrity—more fatal at times than actual wickedness.

Lack of ambition is generally a negative quality that serves as a refuge for incapacity.

It is also the direct proof of distrust in one's own strength, negation of ambition being nearly always the herald of defeat.

It is nothing but vanity ill-disguised, a futile and stubborn form of presumption which keeps its victim from the fight out of fear of defeat— a contingency that would hurt self-love too much.

It happens nearly always that those who assert contempt for ambition punctuate their philosophy by the words, "You see I am not one of Fortune's favorites," or "I am too prone to ill luck to attempt anything like that."

Others add, "I did not dare the attempt because I knew myself to be unlucky."

If they would reflect ever so little before giving way to their monotonous complaints they would see that luck in the proper sense of the word, that is to say that precious vein of gold can only be won by him who can descend into the mine and tear it from the rock which holds it prisoner, or from the earth which conceals it.

He who is doubtful of finding it, or becomes discouraged at the first attempt will never become its possessor.

This thrice-lucky vein of gold will never be found by the timid who fear the dangerous subterranean adventure.

No more will it fall to the rash man, who instead of availing himself of all the precautions known to the gold-seekers' trade, enters maimed upon his task.

It will fall a conquest to those daring ones who, with the aid of ripe judgment seek it under the proper conditions, and who find encouragement in the knowledge that, once discovered, it will assure their future happiness.

CHAPTER V

LUCK AND CHANCE

ALTHO chance quite often partakes of the qualities of luck none but the most superficial would think of confounding the two.

Luck is happy chance produced by the effect of circumstances which we are accustomed to regard under the aspect of fatality.

It is nearly always some isolated circumstance which is denoted by the term.

Believers in luck have established between the isolated manifestation and its repetition a difference which is exprest by two almost similar phrases, whose range of meaning, nevertheless, is quite distinct.

In speaking of one to whom has befallen some lucky chance, the French say, he has had some luck, and they then mention of what it consists.

If they wish to designate one whose life was filled with lucky chances, they say he has had luck.

In the first case they mean that he was visited

by opportunity at the time to which they make reference.

In the second they wish to infer that fortune has been an assiduous, protecting power, appearing upon the slightest occasion, in a word that luck exercised a powerful influence upon the whole life of the person in question.

We can not always put faith in the beneficent intention of those who pay this sort of compliment.

To say that any one has been lucky is not a very high tribute to his intelligence.

To declare that success is due to good luck is often equivalent to denying the qualities of willpower, perseverance, patience and endurance which are the habitual traits of those who succeed.

It is the judgment pronounced upon those whose success is believed to have been usurped.

In letting it be understood that luck is the sole source of their success, the inference is that without such intervention they would have been incapable of succeeding.

We have shown in a preceding chapter how erroneous it is to think that genuine good fortune can come to him who has made no provision for it, or neglected to extend the proper welcome to the distinguished visitor.

Without insisting further upon this point, already sufficiently developed, we would yet draw attention to the error upon which rests the misconception in question.

Luck, or good fortune, does not lack explanation for the reason that it consists of a chain of chance events, each of which is determined by a cause.

Many persons attribute the origin of luck to obscure causes.

They persuade themselves that it is governed by special laws, of which laws they would like to have some explanation.

At times they imagine that they have actually grasped this coveted knowledge by putting together coincidences whose results have been found to be identical.

A certain fact having taken place in a certain way under certain circumstances, they conclude that a repetition of the same conditions will produce an analogous fact.

Again, they think themselves assured against mischance re-occurring within definite limits.

Thus we often hear people say quite seriously: "I feel quite safe in going out to-day because there was an accident yesterday on the road."

And if they are asked how a past event of this

kind can have any effect upon their present
safety they will reply quite confidently: "Oh!
there has never been an instance of the same
accident being repeated the next day."

Upon what do they base their conclusion?

Simply upon the chances of probability.

Yet these chances of probability were quite as
many on the eve of the accident.

If we suppose the number of accidents that
take place in a year to be represented by the
figure X, there is nothing to prove that this
number can not be increased by an unlooked-
for disastrous series; and the catastrophe of the
day before can, under no consideration, be regarded as a guaranty of safety for the morrow.

Nevertheless, those who reason in this wise
are not altogether in the wrong; tho their deduction is entirely false, the conclusion that
follows it may be true.

There is little chance of the same accident
being repeated for the reason that on the morrow
of a catastrophe the super-excited attention of
the public caused by the painful incidents of the
disaster prompts the taking of measures tending
to prevent a repetition.

Later on, when the painful impression is
effaced and the remembrance of the horrors has

faded, there is more likelihood of imprudence or relaxing of authority.

The sole validity in this kind of dicer's security lies in this way of reasoning, and not in the superstition which consists in representing mischance as something sinister not likely to pass twice by the same road.

This belief is as false as the opposite conviction, which consists in hoping that the intervention of good fortune may be brought about if we can but reproduce a certain set of circumstances already known to be propitious.

Good fortune, then, is the result of one or more lucky chance events. But chance itself—is it the product of some occult will?

Is it some powerful divinity?

Is it in reality the blind and capricious entity to which the superstitious pay reverence?

As soon as we abandon the realm of fiction and enter that of reason we perceive that chance is regarded by the intelligent as the fictive cause of a train of circumstances.

It is brought about without organization.

It is the unexpected encounter of the elements which concur in its formation.

Nevertheless, chance never supervenes except as the sequel of a cause.

We shall not enter into the details of the difficult question of causality, but shall content ourselves with merely sketching out its main lines.

Every phenomenon, whether it be called chance, opportunity, or misfortune, has a cause.

This cause is also named the principle.

The principle is the beginning, the genesis of everything.

The cause, taken in another sense, is also the motive.

It is the reason which determines the fact.

We will suppose that a lady in leaving a ball-room has neglected to put on her wraps, and as a consequence has contracted an affection which developed into a long illness resulting in death.

Fétichards will say: "She had the ill luck to take sick and could not be cured."

The dictum of the intelligent will be: "The *cause* of her death was not ill luck, but her own imprudence which made her neglect to take the ordinary precautions. This imprudence determined a cold which was the *principle* of her illness, meaning by that term the beginning of it."

As every one knows, nothing exists without a cause, and everything has a principle, that is to say a beginning.

The cause is also known as the motive; and in this case, while continuing to suggest the idea of origin, it also awakens that of relativity.

The motive of a thing is always coincident with its reason for being.

It is the tie which binds the initial cause to the principle of that thing.

Cause is divided into four principal categories:

First—That cause of which we have just spoken, which is the determining agent.

Secondly—The element from which this cause is drawn.

Thirdly—The idea or the plan conceived as to a given subject.

Fourthly—The ends which it represents and which are called final causes.

All these causes, brought together and grouped under the title of causalities, always constitute the genesis of chance.

Chance is produced by the cooperation of causes.

At times it is difficult to determine these, but they always exist.

This is why those who believe purely and simply in the intervention of a thing, without that thing receiving any outside help, remain powerless to ward off the consequences.

Now if we take the trouble to use our reason, disregarding the while all incitements of moral weakness toward cessation of effort, we shall see that in a given circumstance, when luck makes a sudden entrance upon the stage, its exit will be just as sudden, unless it be accompanied and supported by its satellites who appear in the train of its creation—Will.

There is hardly a newspaper reader who upon seeing the name of the winner of the chief prize in the Lottery, can refrain from exclaiming, "What a lucky man!"

Yet, of all who give way to the exclamation how many are there who know anything about the lucky man's past?

The total of the prize probably does not represent the sums which during the course of years have been swallowed up in the hazardous enterprise.

Attention is confined to the winning ticket only, and the rest are ignored.

The winner of the chief prize is (save for the exception that confirms the rule) the best patron of the lottery, and his luck of the moment is but the compensation for enormous losses.

Experimenters, professing the incredulity as regards luck that marks all sensible men, have at times produced statistics tending to prove the truth of their theory.

They have carefully set apart those who have made an unexpected stroke of luck, and have followed them step by step through their career.

Some, dazzled by fortune and ignorant of the value of money they did not have to earn, let themselves lapse into prodigal courses with the usual result—the vanishing of the fortuitously grasped treasure.

Others have seen in the windfall but the means of gaining great sums without working.

Fortune, however, unseconded by the qualities she demands for her escort, veils her face forthwith and departs for her fabled realm.

Still others, and these are the least to blame, see themselves despoiled by sharpers who in the guise of capitalists take advantage of their inexperience.

We pass over those who become the prey of malefactors or the victims of fatal circumstances.

Statistics show that out of one hundred of those characterized as lucky winners hardly ten escape the common lot, that of waking up some morning to find themselves as poor as ever.

And at this point the partizans of chance will be ready to claim a victory, saying that these ten are the lucky ones, while the others were lacking in the gift.

Truth, however, compels us to contradict them.

These ten are the wise ones; they are the ones who have known how to profit by a lucky chance which they knew how to put to profit, tho they did not bring it about; and we are right in affirming that even without their windfall they would still have reached success.

Fortune, perhaps, would have come to them by a less rapid route, but it would not have failed to respond, as it always does to the obstinate toil of the persevering.

This is what we see clearly defined in what is called the result produced by the cooperation of causes.

This train of circumstances, brought about by a series of efforts converging on a single goal and guided by a directing will, always develops a power which is superior to all the tricks of chance.

At times it becomes the pivot of chance itself.

Fetishists call it luck.

Those whom faith in their own mental powers alienates from what they regard as superstition have named it *recompense*.

The fact is, for those whom healthy reasoning and the habit of deduction have equipped with good judgement, it is quite easy to reconstitute the generating causes of chance.

It will then be recognized that these always bring about the result that logically should flow from them.

We have not yet referred to exceptions which, as one may say with truth, but confirm the rule.

It sometimes happens that events totally unexpected have come from causes that give rise to the suspicion that chance is their author.

If they are of the favorable sort they are crowned with the name of luck; if the contrary kind, they fall under the ban of ill luck.

But what is not sufficiently reflected upon, nor always recognized, is that while the production of these facts is undeniable, it oscillates, within a certain lapse of time, between set-back and success.

The wise are those who, while taking into account the caprices of chance, do everything to render it favorable.

They do not always succeed; this would be asking too much. But they take means to defend themselves against ill fortune by providing in advance against its inroads.

Two men are trapped in a house which is on fire. They rush headlong for the window, the only possible means of escape. It is several stories from the ground. What is to be done?

The flames are gaining on them and they must decide quickly. There is but one choice: either jump or be burned to a cinder.

One seizes the mattress from the bed and drops it to the street just below the window. Then snatching up clothes and curtains, he knots them together and, climbing over the balcony, slips down on them.

Provided the improvised rope be not too short, the fall will be slight and the mattress below will lessen its impact.

There are several chances, then, that the man will light upon the ground more or less hurt but saved from serious injury.

The second has remained in the blazing room, tearing his hair and cursing his tragic fate, while the flames are spreading; impotent, too terrified to make any bold attempt to save himself, and yet frantic at the idea of inevitable death, he recoils till the window is reached. The flames are almost touching him.

The horrible alternative inspires in him an act, instinctive, yet hardly springing from the

instinct of self-preservation. This act, with
the impulsive, consists in precipitating oneself
upon any risk whatever in order to escape an
inevitable danger.

He jumps.

The frightful shock has dislocated his mem-
bers, and he expires in a few moments in the
arms of his companion in misfortune; who, however, by virtue of good judgment and its sequel,
decision, has escaped the catastrophe which was
fatal for the other.

There are persons who will say of the first:
"He had the luck to escape from the fire."

And of the second: "He was not lucky enough
to escape."

All chance events of the evil sort do not permit of our escaping their consequences, and
we do not mean to assert that in these cases it
is always feasible to avoid disaster.

It will be seen upon reflection that in the
example just cited of the man who was saved,
the word *lucky* can only be used in the sense
of relativity.

He saved his life . ut suffered the loss of his
property, and must remain for a time the worse
for his fall.

And here, by the way, we have a striking

ilustration of the difference between chance and luck.

One might say he had the ill luck to be the victim of sorry *mischance*.

The mischance was the fire.

The ill luck was the fact of suffering from it.

By cleverness the suffering was kept within limits.

Now, for the intelligent there is no such thing as ill luck.

Good sense, that priceless possession, always saves them from being delivered and bound hand and foot to that divinity.

He who, while admitting chance, is determined to do what he can to regulate what causes it, as far as this lies in his power, will never allow himself to be ruled by a belief the main result of which is to minister to moral weakness.

He will do all in his power to prevent ill luck from appearing in the guise of sorry mischance, and if it be found impossible to suppress it completely he will do his best to attenuate it and, while bravely enduring it, will cherish the hope of mending it.

CHAPTER VI

THE PART THAT LUCK PLAYS IN LIFE

THOSE who have read the preceding pages with attention will be inclined to believe the part played by luck in life is much less considerable than might first be imagined.

Perhaps it would be just to say that those who would convince us of the contrary are nearly all given to physical indolences or intellectual atony.

It is so easy to let life slide on and to lay to the charge of some obscure entity all the responsibilities we do not care to shoulder ourselves.

It will be remarked, moreover, that the hidebound partizans of the doctrine are the first to deny it just as soon as it touches their vanity.

They are all disposed to attribute their reverses to the ill will of fortune; but let success come, and straightway they attribute it to their own merits.

Luck! That is for others. It applies to their friends, their colleagues, all but themselves who have gained success.

All, in their view, owe the realization of their aims to a train of circumstances so favorable that it would, in truth, have been difficult for them to avoid succeeding.

Ah! if they could only say as much.

But no, ill luck has dogged them remorselessly, they assure us; it has pursued them as persistently as it has avoided their neighbors.

What then is to be done? What can be attempted against an intangible thing which only shows itself in chance encounters?

It is to be noted that persons who thus complain do not neglect to speak with contempt of other's success.

"Yes," they say, "such a one has been raised by luck to the pinnacle of success, nevertheless he did nothing to deserve this good fortune; ah! if I had only been in his place! If, instead of having mischance always clinging to me, I had been favored by his good luck!"

But if fortune, in the guise of some unforeseen opportunity, some day knocks at his door, he will not fail to show his less-favored friends all the disdainful hauteur at his command.

In this instance luck has disappeared; there is no question of complaisant chance here; this result, as brilliant as it was unexpected, has in it nothing whatever of fortuitous character; it is entirely due to his singular merits.

This shallowness marks the greater part of those who, too weak to make a conquest of luck, too indolent to master it and too superficial to sustain it if it visit them, are glad to give a plausible pretext for their neglectfulness.

The evil would be less than one might fear if they could only be brought to realize their bad faith, but in this case persuasion rarely accomplishes its purpose.

By dint of repeating that they are unlucky they end by realizing the suggestion.

Having made these declarations with the unique object of safeguarding pride and as an excuse for indolence, they feel slowly strong in their arguments of self-exculpation.

It does not suffice for them to merit the indulgence of others, they wish to appear innocent to themselves.

The pretext is so easy, it flatters their natural tendencies so much, that the second "ego" accepts with fervor the absolution that the first dictates.

Little by little imagination is converted into reality, and as it is infinitely convenient to yield to one's inclination, while calling it necessity, they wind up by definitely abandoning themselves to their natural weakness, finding excuses the while which lessen and finally kill remorse.

"How," they ask, "can you struggle against a power which fells you to the ground before you know what has struck you. Is it not the wisest cause to dissemble as best one can, and to try to regard as something imprisoned, or to forget, that terrible entity that we name chance."

And, strong in this argument destined to delude them, they sink anew into their torpor.

In addition to these we often meet the exacting sort, who are ever ready to complain of the slightness of the rôle that chance has played in their lives.

These are never satisfied with its intervention no matter how favorable it may have been.

They would like to see it manifest itself upon all occasions of life, and would find it quite natural if chance would assume charge of their personal welfare.

True, no matter how luck may show itself in

their regard they will be found inclined to criticize its acts.

Too coy in some cases, it is too unrestrained in others, and if momentarily it ceases to pour its gifts into their lap they break out in lamentations, forgetful of its past favors.

It is a rare thing if this way of acting is dictated by any other sentiment than extreme indolence, allied to a presumption which will not admit the least inferiority.

This mental attitude is exprest by the familiar saying, "He imagines that he has a right to everything."

It is, in fact, the habitual state of mind of the exacting; nothing that comes to them in the way of happiness astonishes them; no matter how unlikely the thing that befalls them, they regard it as due tribute, indispensable homage to their personal worth.

On the other hand, if chance, badly served by their own carelessness, gives only partial satisfaction, they rise in denunciation against adverse fortune, forgetting all former favors.

Like the indolent, the exacting endure with bad grace the shackles of misfortune; they are unarmed against ill luck, and their equipment does not permit them to foresee it.

Again, we see superstitious persons so intent upon doing away with the idea of ill luck that they will not pronounce its name. With them it is not a question of boldly denying it and asserting the supremacy of will-power. Nevertheless, this very silence proclaims their fetishism.

They regard ill luck as a dangerous enemy that should be allowed to sleep, lest upon awaking it should fall upon the blockhead who roused it from its torpor.

These are the same persons who do not permit themselves to be felicitated on their good fortune. If some one, moved by the best intentions, addresses them in such simple words as, "I congratulate you on your good fortune," they precipitate themselves upon some object to conjure away the bad luck.

Some will touch wood with fervor while pronouncing this formula thrice: "May nothing happen."

In their imagination this invocation is addrest to ill luck, which is exhorted not to appear and is given assurance that it has not been summoned.

Some, upon hearing the word *guigne* (ill luck), crack their fingers and utter their familiar fetish.

Others quickly pull a hair from their head.

This queer action, which must be opportunely performed, is intended to appease the divinity by offering it a sacrifice. The one incurring the slightest suffering is chosen by the votary of superstition who thinks that he has satisfied the evil deity by dedicating to it this infinitesimal pain.

Another obscure idea is latent in this uncouth act. To pull out a hair, to make a sacrifice, slight as it is, in the name of the divinity, is to show it honor and to flatter it by the recognition of its power.

In all fetishists the soul of ancient paganism is revived in its completeness.

What place have reason and self-control in minds wholly occupied with the rubbish of superstitions of the past?

Such a narrow one, no doubt, that these two virtues thus cramped, can hardly be expected to prolong their stay. No more than a flying visit can be expected of them.

Such persons, along with the indolent and the over-exacting, usually become the playthings of the terrible thing they fear. Their plight, moreover, is made worse by the fact that they are impotent to withstand the blows of evil destiny.

The dull of mind, while putting in practise a totally oposite system, hardly show more wisdom in their conduct.

They go right ahead without reflecting, remarking to themselves: "If I have any luck I shall succeed."

Some offer the remark as if it were a very sensible one: "Provided we are left alone by ill luck we have many chances of success."

It is patent that, no matter what the business and howsoever well conducted, one should always take into consideration the unexpected which may possibly appear as catastrophe.

The wise never fail to take account of this possibility and to adopt all necessary precautions against disaster—even if there be nothing in the present that seems to forbode evil.

But the dull of mind, those who take "chances promising success," who are always ready to celebrate their good luck and rejoice in it without perceiving its dangerous aspects—these without exception will become the prey of circumstances for which they have been responsible.

When this moment comes they will cry out against ill luck, accusing it of all the mistakes which in reality are due solely to their own imprudence.

In all the circumstances of life the rôle played by luck can, with a few exceptions, be regulated by good judgment.

We hear every day some such phrase as this *apropos* of the announcement of a wedding: "Marriage is a lottery in which one must have luck in order to draw a prize."

To understand the falseness of this saying all that we have to do is to take the trouble to observe things.

A few minutes given to thinking, based on the appeal of facts of which we are the daily witness will very quickly alter this appreciation.

It is even a matter of necessity to refute it since it threatens the future happiness of young married people, who, if they set up their home with the idea that the peace and happiness of their union rests merely upon chance, will make no effort to attain that end by making the mutual sacrifices that marriage demands.

Mutual study of character, determinative of concessions that must be made on the part of each, will seem to them a negligible thing.

What is the use of taking so much trouble? If they have been lucky enough to draw a good number they can be happy without troubling themselves about all that; if they have been unlucky enough to draw a worthless one, what can they do? Regret it, that's all.

The latter is the case, for the most part, with the mismated; they deplore their ill luck, without perceiving that they increase and multiply the subjects of discontent in giving them an importance that they do not possess in reality. The proverb to the effect that "we find solace for our griefs in telling them" has helped to demoralize more than it has consoled.

The fact is that brooding over griefs revives and renews them. Also must be taken into account that unconscious exaggeration which paints things in the blackest colors in order to excite commiseration.

The expression, " he has lost his head," by its *naïveté* describes well the state of mind of the husband who yields to the temptation to unbosom himself.

If his troubles do not sufficiently impress his confidant he will not hesitate to exaggerate them.

For the most part he is not entirely lacking in good faith either, for he reasons if things have not passed exactly as he represents, it is scarcely the fault of the culprit, who is capable of all that is attributed to him.

Also he does not hesitate to charge to his account all the sins that he supposes he intended to commit.

All this takes place in case of contradiction.

In case the complainer finds a complaisant confidant, things are represented as worse than ever.

The lamenter sees his griefs magnified by his confidant's indignation.

He swiftly begins to reproach himself for not putting his troubles in proper relief.

He admires his own patience, and, sustained by vanity, he issues from the scene of the conversation firmly resolved never to show so much indulgence upon a future occasion.

How many faults of venial nature have, for the reasons we have mentioned, become the ground for strife and final separation.

We must also include in the regrettable results brought about by these outpourings, the factor vanity, one of the most powerful agents of disorder.

There are numbers of married pairs who remain separated because they do not dare to be reconciled before friends to whom they have confided their troubles.

What share, then, does chance take in all this?

It must be confest that it is a very slight one, almost nothing, in fact, if we take the trouble to reason it out.

It is a very frequent thing to see a pair who have been divorced because of supposed frailties of character re-marry and live perfectly happy together.

What becomes of luck in these cases?

We often hear this plaint from a husband who has been divorced: "Ah! I have had no luck in the marriage lottery."

And concerning the same woman one hears this from the lips of her second husband: "It may be said with truth that I have been lucky in the lottery of marriage."

If the conditions are not identical the idea is the same in both cases, and it is not a rare thing to see the second spouse vaunt the qualities of the woman in whom the first partner found only the opposite defects.

Are we to conclude from this that a change was wrought in the woman in such a short time?

Is it not more rational to suppose that these excellent traits always existed in her, but that it was not given to her first husband to discover them?

And if the second has succeeded in doing this

is it due to chance or to his powers of observation and his knowledge of the human heart?

We have said enough, I think, to make it plain that marriage in no way resembles a game of chance. Into this association, involving both body and soul, there is scarcely occasion for chance to intrude.

True, the married are not more shielded than others from the accidents and blows of fortune, but their harmonious *entente* gives them the strength to provide against them if they can not avert them.

Thus, once more, ill fortune is shown to be vanquished by reason and sane guidance.

Feeble natures, those that allow themselves to be influenced by unfavorable incidents, those who have only tears to oppose to the assaults of ill luck, will always find themselves excluded from fortune's favors.

"Two women," says an Eastern tale, "once found themselves in great trouble

"They met and indulged themselves in mutual confidences.

" 'Never,' " said one, 'have I found happiness in my journey; never has it deigned to smile upon me. I have never seen anything but the sinister face of sorrow.'

"With these words she bent over, weeping, and hid her face in a fold of her mantle.

" 'I have as much reason to complain as you,' said the second. 'I have never seen the face of joy, but I have often met misfortune on the road.

" 'Nevertheless,' she added, 'I do not give way to despair, but continue on, keeping my eyes open and ever hoping to see luck rise in my path.'

"The other replied only by sobs.

"Her companion continued: 'Come, we will resume our journey together. We will ask of all we meet whether they have seen happiness pass by, and perchance we shall find it. Take my arm and we will go forward bravely.'

"But her despairing companion contented herself with burying her head in her lap, while she redoubled her tears. Whereupon she who had been speaking merely shrugged her shoulders, and, calling all her courage and will-power to her aid, set off alone.

"As the road turned she glanced back at her unfortunate companion, and saw what struck her with astonishment.

"Before the object of human wretchedness Happiness was passing. For one moment it paused before the prostrate woman, then, with a glance of disdain, passed on.

"The eyes of the woman who had shown such courage were fixt in fascination upon the long dreamed-of form. She advanced straight toward her. Happiness turned and looked at her, and, arrested by the power of that glance, made her a sign to approach."

The whole history of fortune is epitomized in this tale.

What a number of people there are who pretend that fortune has never had part in their lives, and yet these very persons have often had the goddess within arm's length without making the slightest effort to accost her.

Some, like the woman in the story, absorbed in their futile sorrows, are unable even to lift their heads to look around them. Others, seeing the wished-for form afar off, fail to recognize it; while others still lack even the strength to make a sign.

Still more heap curses upon the divinity because she seems to turn aside from, or abandon them. They do not know the virtue of waiting. Opportunity is always passing in the life of man. The thing to do is to keep wide awake in order to recognize and take advantage of it.

If we subject to a serious analysis the lives of those who style themselves the victims of constant misfortune, we shall find that they have been visited by fortune many times; but because welcome and respect were lacking the visits were brief and fruitless.

How many persons there are who denounce as misfortune what others regard as happiness!

The question of relativity is a most important one in the appraisements of those who complain of their lot.

Sometimes a man will declare himself ruined; yet the *débris* of his possessions would mean wealth for some one less exacting.

The figures which for a workman would represent the realization of a life's ambition, would mean a sort of penury for a man used to wealth.

In order that we may appreciate the gifts of fortune we must not demand too much of it.

To count exclusively upon chance's favors in the regulation of life is the part of the indolent and the fool.

Luck is like her sister, Fortune. She smiles on the daring, but loves, above all, the wise and the provident, and takes up her home with them most willingly.

From time to time she permits herself to

VII.7

wander, and crosses the threshold of the fool or good-for-nothing, but has hardly alighted before she takes sudden flight, put to rout by the vices she most abhors.

CHAPTER VII

OPPORTUNITY AND FORTUNE IN THE LIVES OF GREAT MEN

It is customary to say that fortune (luck in ordinary speech) has smiled upon the great men of whom history tells us.

The genesis of most discoveries we are told is to be ascribed to chance.

And examples are cited.

It was by chance, we are assured, that Newton was able to find a relative between the law of universal gravity and the falling of an apple.

This very simple phenomenon was for him the revelation of a principle which had magnificent results for learning, and whose application was to be of vast utility to man.

If we take the trouble to think for a moment we shall perceive that if the falling apple had not been noticed by one well-equipped for the study of the problem, nothing unusual would have happened.

Even now, when the anecdote is known to all, we see apples falling every day in the orchard without having our thoughts drawn to the law of gravity, which, nevertheless, is being actually illustrated for us.

It must have been, then, that the philosopher had been making ready for this chance event by long study and constant application.

It was because the incident of the falling apple harmonized with his meditations upon nature's mysteries that it had importance, and that from this ordinary incident came a ray of light which furnished the solution of what he had been seeking for so long.

It has often been told how Christopher Columbus was upon the eve of making his great discovery when his demoralized crew threatened to mutiny.

If three days more had been allowed to pass without land being found we are assured that the great navigator would have been murdered by the sailors who were eager to give up a futile expedition and to return home.

If they failed in their design it was because Columbus begged them to be patient for a few hours more, when he swore that he would show them land.

Before the time expired land appeared as a line of blue upon the horizon.

And luck is the conclusion.

Not at all. Luck had nothing to do with it. It was the recompense of great strength of character joined to brilliant gifts of observation.

When Columbus promised his companions that they should see land, he knew that it could not be far off from the fact that he had noticed grass floating upon the waves.

With the accuracy of judgment that characterizes all his acts he concluded that the *débris* indicated the near presence of vegetation.

The discovery of land, then, was not a stroke of luck on his part, but rather the culmination of heroic efforts accomplished by magnificent courage and power of observation, which are at the root of all famous achievements.

What we call luck often means calmness in seizing opportunities.

But this aptitude involves qualities of observation whose starting-point is strength of character and of will, traits which permit of the coolness and clear-headedness necessary to the successful and practical discoverer.

The indolent are always found complaining of their ill luck, which they say never puts an opportunity within their reach.

Those who are determined to succeed are

always encountering opportunities, and are in the habit of seizing them with eagerness and of lying in wait for more.

For all those men who have left their name in history will, perseverance, and activity of mind have been the generators of their so-called luck.

Sometimes those who do not possess these qualities find themselves face to face with opportunity, but they seldom perceive it, or, at most, get little profit from it, for they do not know how to make the right use of it.

It is true that it does not always present itself rounded out and complete; it is not always the brilliant butterfly which lights upon the hand of those it singles out, filling them for an instant with pleasure by its splendid appearance.

It is more frequently a larva which the stupid and the ignorant crush under foot without perceiving.

The indolent, indeed, sometimes remark it, but they recoil before the effort needed to achieve it.

Before making the attempt they resolve in their minds the long time required for development, the risks involved, and they shrink from the series of acts essential for the desired transformation.

They like to persuade themselves that their energies will be superfluous, that they will represent pure loss, and they console themselves for letting opportunity pass by with these words which every man of character should erase from his vocabulary: "It can not succeed."

Excusing inertia results in aggravating it and rendering it habitual.

Those who have known definitive success are those who have never doubted success.

We may wonder, indeed, how they have escaped discouragement at the numerous checks in the course of their efforts toward success, for as we know, every achievement is accompanied by inconveniences and mistakes.

Those who have reached the goal certainly have not been exempt from these trials; but the latter have in no way weakened their courage. Instead of charging up their mistakes to the account of some shadowy, inimical being called luck, they examine carefully into their causes and take measures to provide against them for the future.

If those whose names have been transmitted to us by posterity have succeeded in acquiring fame it is because they obeyed the laws upon which every successful achievement rests.

They first examined with great care the idea which contained the germ of the enterprise.

They thus gained a careful estimate of the possibilities of success involved in the achievement.

It was only when they arrived at the conviction of possible success that they were brought to regard the enterprise in question as worthy of their serious efforts.

At the moment of favorable decision they devoted themselves completely to the project, taking into consideration the slightest details bearing on the subject and drawing profit from whatever experience has taught.

Should it astonish us if one out of all these events involved in the undertaking should turn out to be the source of success? Or can we, with any show of reason, suppose that the successful achievement may be ascribed to the influence of some beneficent entity whose potency is paramount to all the qualities which we have described?

If Jenner had not kept his mind centered upon a single aspiration we should be ignorant to-day of the benefits of vaccine.

He was quite young, still a student, when one day a countrywoman called to consult him.

The heavy fever which was upon her caused the future physician to suspect small-pox, a disease then widespread.

"It is impossible," said she, "because I have already had the cow-sickness."

Jenner was interested. He learned that in this young woman's country people who had caught a form of infection from the cows looked on themselves as immune from the disease. There was not one of these, she told him, who ever became the prey of the small-pox.

Jenner's attention was instantly fixt upon this fact of observation, neglected by others, and he set himself to discover what truth there was in it.

One may see in the visit of the peasant and her exclamation the intervention of luck.

Certainly, it was a chance of happy import, but had not this very chance been offered before to physicians who had neglected their opportunity?

However that may be, strength of will and perseverance were essential for developing the possibilities of the chance event.

We will not record here the years spent in observation, the years of struggle that marked the career and final triumph of the scientist.

Like all innovators, he had to combat routine and obscurantism.

But in his case the opposition encountered was particularly difficult to overcome, since it came, not from the public only, but from those charged with the task of enlightening it.

Vaccination was stigmatized from the pulpit as an invention of the devil.

The people, amplifying, according to custom, the impression received, instantly gave credence to the most uncouth stories about the discovery.

Many averred that the newly vaccinated became marked with protuberances on the forehead, indicating the place for horns, and that their voices became hoarse like the lowing of cows.

Jenner fought twenty years to imbue the mind of his contemporaries with the conviction which animated him.

When, at the close of his life, he received his compensation in wealth and honors, would any one have the hardihood to say that it was all done through luck?

In this case it must be confest that the favored one did much to push his luck.

Many of the partizans of fetishism have upheld Bernard Palissy as an example of what luck

can do for a man. The artist's house was almost
reduced to *débris* when he came upon the discovery of the casting of enamel; a few hours
more, and the great artist, up to his ears in debt
and denuded of nearly everything, would have
been overwhelmed and beyond the possibility of
making further efforts.

Perhaps in his case it is true that luck gave
aid; but it must be admitted that he accomplished the impossible, and that almost any one
else in his place would have lost courage before
well-deserved opportunity came to the rescue.

The invention of porcelain of Saxony might
also be attributed to chance by the superficial
observer. Yet if we examine into the history of
this invention we shall find it characterized by
a sort of fury of application and perseverance.

Boettcher was in the service of the grand
elector of Saxony, who hoped to obtain from
his discoveries a method of transmuting material. The scientist was trying to find out how
potter's clay could be transformed into porcelain, and applied himself to a study of the required composition, but without entire success.

Some vases imported from China which he
had seen inspired him with a desire to imitate
the art of the Orientals.

He set to work eagerly but his efforts were not crowned with success, and he had begun to despair when one day, noticing that his peruke felt too heavy, he bethought himself to examine the powder that it was covered with.

Kaolin was thus discovered; and herein was the origin of the production, as artistic as it is remunerative, of the magnificent porcelains of Saxony which are immensely admired.

The rôle of luck is here confounded with that of chance. Nonetheless, if we reflect upon the incident we shall see how the power of a directing thought can be discerned in this superb result.

How many inventors, less sharp-witted and industrious, would have contented themselves with simply shaking the powder out of the wig, without ever thinking of examining it?

Great generals have no more been spared than others by fetishists, who have hastened to put the tag of luck upon them.

There are to be found many people who hold that Napoleon counted largely on luck throughout his life.

It is certain that the entrance of this genius upon the scene coincided with political storms which permitted him to carve out for himself

a place commensurate with his greatness in a
country disorganized by the Terror and invaded
by the foreigner.

Under another *régime,* he, perhaps, would
never have become emperor, but he would have
been spared the Calvary of Saint Helena.

No less certain is it that if Napoleon had
the luck, so to speak, to be born in an age in
which his genius could have full career, he knew
how to profit by this luck and to achieve success
of an incomparable kind.

It would be impossible to find a more striking
example of strength of character and indomita-
ble will. By constructing the road of the Sim-
plon, he literally conquered the Alps.

He pretended that he had erased the word
"impossible" from the French dictionary; and
all his pretensions had the vindication of being
transformed into facts.

His life furnishes the refutation of superstitious belief in an obscure power acting in
ignorance of us and directing our acts.

His contemporaries called him not "the glori-
ous," but "the organizer of glory."

His power of willing radiated, as it were,
from him and transformed uncertainties into
facts.

For the simple-minded this man, who seems the elect of Fortune, has become an actual fetish; his story electrifies them and prompts them to heroic acts.

It would be impossible to find a more striking example of sustained power of will and coherence of ideas.

In another order of ideas we find attracting our notice the celebrated explorer, Livingstone, who began his career as a workman in a Glasgow cotton-mill.

The unenterprising will be inclined to declare that it was pure luck that gave Livingstone his opportunity for fame. But do they realize how hard it was to deserve this luck?

Without neglecting his work he educated himself by his own efforts, saving enough out of his wages to buy the necessary books.

It was thus that he made his studies in medicine and won his degree as licentiate.

We will not speak of his life, wholly devoted as it was to enterprises full of danger; but in the appreciation of the fame which he won it will be freely granted that his personal worth weighed equally in the scale with fortune.

One might fill volumes with authentic biographies of those to whom has come, unperceived and unused, fortune in the form of chance opportunities. But it is only the subtle and the gifted who have known how to seize and put to advantage those opportunities which, taking root in fertile brains, sometimes arrive at such magnificent fruition.

Would the same things have happened if these opportunities had appeared in the lives of the indolent?

We certainly have the right to affirm the contrary, for we know well that fortune, in whatever guise it may choose to appear, always ignores those who do not know how to put it to good use.

CHAPTER VIII

HOW TO CONQUER FORTUNE

WE have proved sufficiently, I think, that what is called luck or good fortune is not as fortuitous in character as fetishists proclaim it to be.

If it be not always possible to hasten its appearance, it is beyond doubt that one need never despair, for it never fails to give itself up to the eager solicitation of the one who knows how to attract it.

To experience its good effects, however, it is not merely a question of recognizing it the moment it appears and being in readiness to receive its favors.

The feeble and the impotent also do this.

Persons of strong character know how to arrest it, to bend it to their will, in a word to subjugate it.

These are not the slaves of fortune, but its masters.

The most efficacious means of conquering fortune have two essential divisions: moral qualities and physical influences.

The moral qualities may be thus denominated: alertness of comprehension, discernment, decision, knowledge of moral and material values, patience, initiative, and activity, whether effective or latent.

Alertness of comprehension is an indispensable quality for the proper estimating of the importance and range of an event as representing, determining, or engendering opportunity.

As will be easily recalled by glancing at the preceding chapters, good fortune or opportunity rarely presents itself to us under the aspect of complete success.

At times it is hard enough to recognize it, and it requires great alertness of mind to handle properly an event which can only be regarded as fortunate or opportune, provided we can bring it into the right relationship with the object that it is our desire to accomplish.

Alertness of mind gives the immediate representation of the advantages resulting from a fact which, in the case of those not so well equipped, would not be noticed.

It is by neglecting slight details, the importance of which seems to them but secondary, that

the unintelligent or the nonchalant miss culti-
vating the seed that contains in germ the series
of lucky chances that we call fortune.

Sometimes fortune presents itself in an un-
accustomed guise or shows us several aspects of
itself, leaving to us the task of discovering the
right one.

Here discernment comes into play.

Discernment is the act of choosing a determined line of action, the preference being based
on good judgment.

Those who have power of discernment dis-
card without hesitation doubtful chances and
center their efforts upon the ones that seem to
contain the promise of realizing the object of
their pursuit.

This choice, however, should in nearly all
cases be the object of rapid decision, for lack
of preciseness is the enemy of success.

Floating resolutions nearly always meet with
some check.

The man who can not reach a decision, however imperfect, who is always sketching out a
plan which he abandons directly for another,
will never know success.

If we have made allusion to resolutions of imperfect character it is because there are very

few such that do not involve inconvenient features.

For thinkers the happiest solution always includes some risk, and even the germ of danger.

Those, however, who are practised in prompt resolution can make a rapid calculation of the sum of advantages and difficulties; a simple mental subtraction will suffice to dictate their decision which once taken must be stoutly maintained in face of all circumstances.

In the cerebral operation which precedes the decision, as well as in the acts which affirm it, knowledge of values is of paramount importance.

In the attainment of all good things the question of relativity plays the chief rôle.

It is only in rating things at their true value that it is possible to assign to them a rank among the favorable possibilities, which possibilities must always outnumber the doubtful chances.

It is only in studying the coincidences and relations of things that it is possible to estimate them at their proper value. What is very desirable for some things is negligible for others.

On the other hand, there are things ordinarily of no account, which under certain circumstances take on paramount importance and become the starting-point of success, altho they are regarded by the profane as mere strokes of luck.

To the knowledge of moral values it is indispensable that we conjoin the knowledge of material values.

Above all, money should be made the object of a sensible study, to which should be brought whatever aid reason and conversation can supply.

The science of economy is the most powerful auxiliary of luck.

To know the value of money, in the sense that this makes it possible to obtain it, has been the starting-point of all the undertakings which have been regarded as favored by fortune.

Knowledge of the value of money is productive of independence; it is the secret of that serenity of mind which is essential to all success.

Secure possession of a competence prevents the possibility of financial embarrassment with all its attendant evils; it frees the mind from petty cares whose multiplicity saps the founts of intelligence; it banishes discouragement and forestalls the wilfulness that comes of rebellion.

It is not, of course, our intention to praise parsimony. To amass money in order to satisfy the desires of avarice is vile and futile; but to

save in order to provide against the exigencies
of the future is a sign of strength of character,
which backs up pride with providence.

Fortune seldom smiles on the prodigal (except
perhaps in an intermittent fashion), for she
knows well that her favors will be wasted in
useless dissipation.

These are seen to implore vainly the return
of the divinity who, tho she had the weakness
to just touch them, quickly took to flight at
sight of their conduct.

What success, indeed, can reasonably be expected by a prodigal who through imprudence
finds himself outmatched in the race, whether
impotent to fulfil his engagements or handi-
capped by debt?

How can he pretend to dictate to others who
must needs seek support himself?

Economy, rightly understood, has been known
to be the starting-point of many successful ventures; it is also the secret of many successes
which are attributed to chance alone. It as-
suredly is the certain means of holding success
captive, for the consciousness of material independence gives to its possessors a clearness of
judgment that can not be enjoyed by those
harassed by material cares.

It we can not find cause for saving in reason we ought to be able to find it in pride.

Luck loves not the humble, and, like its sister Fortune, it has a weakness for the audacious who never yield to the wretched compromises to which want of money impels the loose-living and the prodigal.

Knowledge of values concerns more than mere money and the relations of things, it also bears very largely upon the question of the value of time.

Time in the sense that it can not be replaced may be regarded as more valuable than money itself.

He who fritters away his time in doing useless things or who lets the hours pass in inaction is as much a fool as one who refining gold in the bed of a river should let precious gold dust filter through the sieve.

He may indeed get back precious particles thus lost, but those which have been caught in the current he can never hope to recover.

It is the same with the moments we squander; the current of life bears them away and they vanish without leaving any trace of their presence.

Contempt of the value of time brings also in

its train inexactitude; now luck does not like waiting.

It does not like to be first at the rendezvous; and, finding no one there, it leaves straightway.

Punctuality is the homage it prefers, and it rarely returns to the rendezvous where it has met disappointment.

Time is the only form of wealth that can be parcelled out equally to all; some there are who squander their treasure without profit to themselves or others.

Certain persons, on the contrary, understand the importance of the capital that has been entrusted to them, and they act the same with time as with money; they never invest it except at good interest.

If it be impossible for them to invest it literally, they capitalize what it represents; each hour is devoted to some useful work and they regain the time spent in the form of some achievement.

The indolent, laggards, those who are interested in idle pursuits hardly ever encounter opportunity, for the reason that they neglect to keep their appointment with it.

It is in vacant hours that ill luck finds its advantage; useful, healthful occupations frighten it away, for it does not tarry among the active.

Ill luck also haunts the impatient, who do not know how to wait for success. For to win it is not enough to put in action the qualities we have named; it is also essential to arm oneself with patience in order to await their happy results.

For those who have toiled confidently and who, having promptly discovered the fact bearing the germs of success, have employed all the means for its development, there remains a formidable danger—impatience.

In trying to hasten the event they compromise the result and render futile all preceding effort.

More strength of mind is needed for awaiting with calmness a hoped-for result than would be required for the several steps of the enterprise itself.

Expectancy is strength, while useless agitation is a source of weakness.

It is essential that we discern the dangers of a given act which, in certain cases, may be attenuated by a wise use of moderation and prudence—virtues all the more meritorious because they are those of the spectator of the events.

Satisfactions of too precocious a nature too often mar the future.

It is the part of discernment to know the attitude imposed by circumstances.

At times it is necessary to consummate an act of audacity, but long patience and the science of opportune expectancy are always essential factors in the problem.

For the rest, it is futile to say that by the word expectancy we merely mean the repression of headstrong volition, for he who knows how to find opportunity and profit by it never remains completely inactive.

His apparent leisure veils an inner energy and unity of aspiration which go to strengthen the salient traits—alertness of understanding and appreciation of values.

This momentary arrest of action may even be fruitful of opportunity for the reason that it permits of concentration, a trait not always within the scope of action.

Contemplation of the idea, providing, as it does, isolation from outward things, favors reflection and makes visible faults not easily perceived in the tumult of action.

It also keeps our thoughts from being scattered, and while guiding them to safety it prevents the interference of parasitical ideas which are always of derogatory nature.

Finally, expectancy permits of collecting and deploying new forces for the purpose of entering the struggle whose prize is fortune.

Hardly less important in this connection are physical influences which have a certain repercussion on the moral nature.

And above all else in importance must be set the influence of words.

No one is ignorant of the striking effect which is produced by the enumeration of certain words of evocative character.

Repeating words suggestive of confidence is a sure way of calling forth that sentiment.

There arises from vocables frequently repeated a suggestiveness that it would be foolish to deny.

The remark, "I will succeed," made opportunely, and marking invincible conviction, will strengthen resolution and make straight the way for the much-desired visit of fortune.

All-powerful is the magic of words.

Some words awaken in us feelings of patriotism, others set in vibration the chords of sentiment, others fill the soul with bitterness.

This is why those who would woo success ought never to pronounce, even mentally, words of doubt.

On the contrary, they should give utterance to words suggestive of what they desire. They should refuse to give way to protestations against mischance, and instead of saying bluntly, "I have bad luck," they ought to put it this way: "My luck has not yet arrived, *but it will come and can not help coming.*"

This sort of courage has a reassuring effect upon the mind and tends to renew its ardor for the coming struggle.

The impression produced by external things is also an important factor in success.

The unlovely character of the age we live in can not fail to shed over our lives the dull tints of melancholy and doubt.

The potency of atmosphere and of color is so real that we currently associate a given state of mind with the *nuance* that awakens an analogous feeling.

We say: "I see life in rose colors," or "I see life in black," according to the nature of our hopes and aspirations.

There is even such a thing as a concordance of colors and sentiments: "To live in the sky" (*être en bleu*) signifies happiness of sentimental nature.

By the "white and black" of existence is

meant life without relief, whose monotony is un-
tinted with any definite joy.

"To grind in black" (*broyer du noir*) is an
expression indicative of despair.

A common expression applied to one who has
given way to some tragic act is: "He sees red."

Finally, white is the color which synthesizes
all the ideas of innocence and purity.

It is not, therefore, the part of temerity to
conclude that the aspect of surrounding things
exercises an influence upon the moral nature
even to the point of determining to some extent
its manifestations.

Those who would take luck captive ought
therefore to enliven their homes and make them
as attractive as possible.

Mischance seldom haunts thresholds adorned
with flowers or homes that re-echo to the sound
of laughter.

In default of joyousness that circumstances
will not always permit of, a tranquil serenity
will keep off the unwelcome visitor more effec-
tively than any exorcism can.

The would-be conqueror of fortune must not
forget that slavery, when made too hard to endure, always verges on rebellion.

It is only by first sounding for it, then bringing it to light, and finally acclimatizing it that we can hope to obtain final possession of it.

The time is then ripe for us to act as master.

To dominate circumstances, to guide the course of chance, to foresee its caprices and obtain some of its smiles—all this is directed toward the conquest of fortune.

To conquer fortune means to put a bit upon capricious fate, to direct events and correct destiny, which, in spite of all the fetishists pretend, is apt to bend to the commands of him whom it recognizes as master.

CHAPTER IX

FORTUNE'S FLUCTUATIONS

FORTUNE was represented by the ancients under the symbol of a blind woman lightly turning a wheel with her foot.

The intention was to indicate the rôle of chance by the sudden starting and pausing of the wheel.

It used to be said of him who could succeed in stopping this eternal fugitive, that "he had put a nail in the wheel of Fortune"; which was equivalent to saying that he had made it so that it would no longer turn, thus preventing its further progress.

An analogous metaphor was used in reference to any one who had been clever enough to arrest the course of the inconstant deity. Of such a one it was said, "he has shackled fortune."

It is sufficiently evident from folk-lore and from the wisdom of nations as it is summed up in proverbs that belief in a fluctuating fortune has always existed with differences of degree and kind; this varying lot assigned to mortals has been known under the names of Fortune, Chance, and in recent times Luck (*la Veine*).

Certain writers find a more exact illustration of the last by comparing it to the undulations of the sea which, tho irregular, are of certain character.

Luck they aver has, like the ocean, incessant waves which advance toward and recede from the shore.

Now there are some who can never manage to be upon the scene at flood tide; they lose patience while waiting for the tide to come in, and they leave before high-water mark is reached. Their arrival is always wrongly timed.

These people are all ready to swear that the sea has never washed the shores they inhabit, and they envy their neighbors who are lucky enough to be able to sport among the waves with the solid sand for a bottom.

Have we not here an image of those who waste their time in complaining and are wont to declare without perceiving the absurdity of it: "I have never met with any luck," or " I have been pursued all my life by ill luck."

Misfortune on such a scale as this has never existed, and if it were possible to piece together the whole life of these minions of ill luck it

would be found that with half of their luck a
man of any cleverness might amass a fortune.

Their name is legion who do not know the
favorable moment to put their boat to sea with
the certainty of returning with their nets full.

Can they in good faith accuse fate if they have
failed to rise with the dawn and put to good use
the propitious hours of morning

All those who give way to plaints about their
persistent *bad luck* resemble these lazy fisher-
men.

They lie unconsciously, and yet their lie is
actual when they maintain that they have never
known opportunity.

No life is entirely devoid of joy, and there is
no one who at some time or other has not been
visited by prosperity.

It is simply a question of imitating the fisher-
man by waiting for the right moment to embark
—that moment when the wind is calmest and all
promises security. Next must come activity,
discernment, and patience, all concurring in the
success of the enterprise.

On some days the catch is certain to be poor;
on others the small fry will exceed the take of
large fish; but the day will come when the fish-
ermen will return triumphant, their boat filled

to overflowing and their families' welfare thus assured.

Luck and ill luck, in most lives, when weighed in the scale should about balance each other. What each one must do is to cooperate with the first and try to parry the blows of the second.

It is well to recall here the parable of the fat and lean cows, and to fill the bin while the luck is in the ascendant in order to provide against a rainy day.

Sometimes it happens that luck comes in the wake of ill luck, connecting it and, as it were, bringing good out of evil.

A very old man, who had no near relations left, resolved to make a will in favor of the son of one of his friends whose good qualities had attracted him.

Finding himself unwell, he besought the young man to have his lawyer come next day in order that he might make an absolutely safe will.

The state of mind of the expectant heir may be imagined, when upon presenting himself with the legal official on his arm at his friend's door he was met by a surly relative who apprized him that the man who intended to enrich him had died suddenly.

VII.9

The law not taking an account of an intention, however formal, the would-be heir must needs retrace his steps, a prey to a double sorrow— his friend's death and his own cruel disappointment.

Without question we may consider this man a veritable victim of bad luck, and it is certain that most persons in his position would have given way under the terrible blow.

But this particular young man was full of energy; renouncing at once all the caressing hopes that had lured him he set out forthwith for the gold country.

The fortune which he had been robbed of he refound in the form of a vein of gold, and inspired by the principles which we have been inculcating, he set to work to make the best of his find.

After a number of years of hard labor intelligently pursued, he returned to his country a rich man, owing his fortune to himself alone.

All this time the heirs who had supplanted him having received their inheritance, the greater part of which consisted of vineyards, were called on to face a disastrous loss caused by the plague called phylloxera.

The wealth they had received from the dead

man, and their own possessions as well, were entirely eaten up.

The wine-stock devastated by the plague was worthless, and when the traveler returned to his native place he found the heirs ruined.

When he saw what had happened he actually felt gratitude for the ill luck which had relieved him of an illusory fortune and put him in the way of gaining a real one.

If what he regarded as ill luck of the most lugubrious kind had not come to him, if death had not intervened to prevent the generous impulse of the testator, he would now be ruined, and at the age when attempts that require daring are no longer possible.

Daily we see examples of these disastrous chances which seem to deserve the name of real luck and yet are fraught with consequences of evil.

A wretched woman holding her child by the hand is run down by an automobile and cruelly injured. This misfortune, nevertheless, becomes the starting-point of prosperity for these poor people. The owner of the car happens to be a conscientious man. He cares for the victims of the accident and, attracted by the child, he provides for it and for the welfare of the whole family.

A certain famous painter owed his success to the ruin of his family who, while they had their little competence, forbade him to occupy himself with what they called a futile art, their desire being that he should become an employee in the public service.

The list would be interminable if we tried to cite all the cases in which good fortune showed itself in the form of mischance.

Even the weak do not fail, under certain circumstances, to derive advantage from misfortune.

They represent ill fortune under the lineaments of an evil personality whose sole occupation is to make them suffer.

And the worst of it is they are convinced of the truth of this theory.

They declare themselves subject to some malediction and proclaim the vanity of their undertakings.

Certain careless individuals wishing to find some excuse for their laziness feign to believe in fate. Luck will come some time, they aver, and that time will be when it pleases. And if it is ill luck that comes instead, what is the use of making any effort when everything is determined in advance?

This process of reasoning seems to excuse their nullity of will, and they like to repeat the well-known line:

"He gives the little birds their food."

But the observing, while respecting the noble sentiment of the great poet, do not fail to remark that the birds always meet with disaster unless the parent birds provide for the wants of their young.

And they conclude that it is well to cooperate with Providence whether it be represented under the aspect of the divine or that of chance.

Also it is the part of the sensible to seize upon chance instead of sinking into apathy which finds its account in calumniating fortune instead of profiting by it.

Neither should those be imitated who reproach the beneficent divinity for failing to respond to their whims and leaving them in the lurch at the critical moment.

Such as these will never be present when the tide is at the flood. They are fated never to embark upon successful expeditions, and they will round out their days in rancor and regret.

Sensible men, on the contrary, who despise indolence and do everything with some object in view, arm themselves according to circumstances with energy, patience, mildness and strength.

Full of that faith of which it has been said that it moves mountains, they may await the hour of fortune, confident that it will always come and that no mortal ever yet has been disbarred from the circle of its beneficence.

They know well that if the ordinary sources of ill fortune are found in wilfulness and vacillation, the active factors of success are found in confidence, energy, patience and action.

HOW TO ARGUE AND WIN

By GRENVILLE KLEISER
Author of "How to Speak in Public."

NINETY-NINE MEN in a hundred can argue to one who can argue and win. Yet upon this faculty more than any other depends the power of the lawyer, business man, preacher, politician, salesman, and teacher. The desire to win is characteristic of all men. "Almost to win a case," "Almost to close a sale," "Almost to make a convert," or "Almost to gain a vote," brings neither satisfaction nor success.

In this book will be found definite suggestions for training the mind in accurate thinking and the power of clear and effective statement. It is the outcome of many years of experience in teaching men "to think on their feet." The aim throughout is practical, and the ultimate object a knowledge of successful argumentation.

CONTENTS

Introductory—Truth and Facts—Clearness and Conciseness—The Use of Words—The Syllogism—Faults—Personality—The Lawyer—The Business Man—The Preacher—The Salesman—The Public Speaker—Brief-Drawing—The Discipline of Debate—Tact—Cause and Effect—Reading Habits—Questions for Solution—Specimens of Argumentation—Golden Rules in Argumentation.

12mo, Cloth.   *$1.25, net; by mail, $1.35.*

FUNK & WAGNALLS COMPANY, Publishers
NEW YORK AND LONDON

SUCCESSFUL SELLING

By E. LEICHTER

A practical treatise which covers the various essentials of selling efficiency in an interesting, inspiring, and yet common-sense manner. The every-day, practical salesman, as well as the "greenest" novice, will enjoy and profit by this sensible book. Out of years of experience the author analyzes and explains every phase of selling. His chapter headings are: The Modern Aspect of Selling; Requisite Qualities; The Approach; The Presentation; The Closing; Negations; The Larger Sale; The Story of a Career.

Leslie's Weekly says it is "a small but valuable book filled with the meat of practical common-sense hints in the art of selling."

Price, 50 cents, net; by mail, 54 cents

FUNK & WAGNALLS COMPANY, Publishers
NEW YORK and LONDON